PRAISE FOR C
PASS W

T0160968

"Cooper is deep, he searcl. ...., ιειates through different forms, different voices, an emotional gravitas as the only constant. *Pass with Care* is moving in both senses of the word."
> **—SARAH SCHULMAN,** author of *Maggie Terry, The Cosmopolitans, Conflict Is Not Abuse,* and others

"*Pass with Care* is a memoir of becoming . . . from working-class kidhood to '90s dyke utopia to life of letters, I cheered this hero on at every turn."
> **—MELISSA FEBOS,** author of *Whip Smart* and *Abandon Me*

"Cooper Lee Bombardier's tender and fierce writing brings class and gender, art and life together with big heart and tough intelligence. [I] am so excited to watch *Pass with Care* enter our crucial contemporary canon."
> **—MICHELLE TEA,** author of *Astro Baby, Against Memoir, Black Wave,* and others

"*Pass with Care* is an insightful trans memoir. It's also a brilliant book about ambivalence, class in America, self-acceptance, discovery."
> **—CHRIS KRAUS,** author of *Summer of Hate* and *After Kathy Acker*

"*Pass with Care* pairs heart-in-hand vulnerability with the split-knuckle candor of venerated queer voices like Dorothy Allison and Saeed Jones . . . gritty as a classic honkytonk song, and as unforgettable, too."
> **—LILY BURANA,** author of *Grace for Amateurs: Field Notes on a Journey Back to Faith, I Love a Man in Uniform,* and *Strip City*

PASS WITH CARE

MEMOIRS

Cooper Lee
Bombardier

dottir
press
NEW YORK CITY

Published in 2020 by Dottir Press
33 Fifth Avenue
New York, NY 10003

Visit www.dottirpress.com

First printing May 2020
Design and production by Drew Stevens

Trade Distribution through Consortium Book Sales
and Distribution, www.cbsd.com.

Library of Congress Cataloging-in-Publication Data is available for this title.

ISBN 978-1-948340-21-2 (Paperback Edition)
ISBN 978-1-948340-48-9 (Hardcover Edition)

CONTENTS

This book is dedicated to Kris Kovick.
It all would have been so much better with you here.

See Beams Glitter

"I've seen things you people wouldn't believe."

In one of the works collected in this gentle, fierce, and highly readable anthology of autobiographical writings, Cooper Lee Bombardier riffs on that famous line by Rutger Hauer as the android Roy Batty in Ridley Scott's dystopian sci-fi classic *Blade Runner*—a perennial touchstone for the trans perception of being uncannily different from our human cis-kin. As Batty's allotted span of life ebbs away, he yearns to convey what it means to have seen "attack ships on fire off the shoulder of Orion," and to have "watched C-beams glitter in the dark near the Tannhäuser Gate." All those moments will be lost in time, he says, like tears in rain, when he dies. And then he dies.

Unlike the fictional Batty, the flesh-and-blood Bombardier has never been off-world, and the unbelievable things he says he's seen "are largely composed of small wonders, fleeting joys, and fragments of human behavior filtered through the lens of being seen as entirely one gender and then another. In the constellations of gender I've traversed, I've seen things that people who presume gender as fixed, innate, and unmoving would never conceive of as possible." Rather than evoking the grand pathos of dying, his words point us toward the humble grace to be found in the persistence of living. For now. Just for now.

I shared a gender constellation with Cooper a quarter-century ago in San Francisco. Those might not have been C-beams glittering in the darkness of dykey dive bars along a pre-gentrified Valencia Street, but something fabulous sure lit up the night down there, back then. Bombardier was one of the bright spots, in my opinion, pretty much from the moment he hit town in 1993. I'd see him hanging out at Red Dora's Bearded Lady Café, in the audience for a Harry Dodge and the Dodge Brothers set at Club Confidential, and interning at Black and Blue Tattoo, where I had some of my own inkwork done. I watched him perform his debut spoken-word piece "Lips like Elvis" for the TransCentral performance series at The Lab, an experimental art incubator in the Mission in 1997, and I remember thinking that this new crop of trans and genderqueer kids was gonna be all right.

Nostalgia is an easy trap to trip on. Whenever I think about "Trans SanFrisco" in the queer '90s, I constantly ask myself whether it could really have been as cool as I remember it feeling when I was living it. And I keep coming to the conclusion that *yeah, I think it really was*. I'd spent my teens and twenties mournful that I'd missed out on the psychedelic '60s, and was still a little too young and definitely too far away from New York's Downtown East Side to have been part of the punk scene in its heyday. For those of us who had genders that were not made for the world we grew up in, being in San Francisco in the early '90s felt like stepping through a rip in the fabric of space-time into some new dimension of possibility. *And we had torn it open ourselves.* For the first time in my life, it felt like I was where something was *happening.* That I was part of it. That we were alive, becoming free, re/making a world by how we moved through it.

I read Cooper's words in the pages of this book and take comfort in knowing that I am not alone in my sense of the consequence of that time and place. Trans SanFrisco in the '90s was a thing. Its history has yet to be written, but the essays in this book are a great place to start. They document something that was not always pretty. It was before the retroviral cocktails made HIV infection something other than a near-term death sentence; friends and lovers left those of us who survived far too soon. For the first time since Vietnam, we were in a hot war, and clearly saw the connections between the overseas violence of the American Empire and that same Empire's domestic violence towards us as queer and trans people, who were still explicitly criminalized and excluded from large swaths of life. When the Cold War ended with the collapse of the Soviet Union, an unfettered global capitalism—embodied in the tech boom—exulted in a new-found fantasy of limitlessness that started lifting real estate prices in San Francisco toward the stratosphere; it brought the increasing unlivability of the New World Order home intimately, one increasingly insufficient paycheck at a time. People had to leave. Cooper did.

What I see most in these pages is not what Cooper left behind, but what he took with him from those halcyon days, when, as he puts it, "our permutations variegated faster than any taxonomy could pace." A quarter-century later, I see in his mature writing a confidence that comes from knowing early in life that what is possible can sometimes become real through our actions. I see intensity, invention, playfulness, persistence, openness. I see a sense of calm. Those are powerful attributes to cultivate and share in a world where what gender means and does still needs to change, along with so much else that needs to change, and which must be survived in the meantime.

I read Cooper Lee Bombardier's words and I see the beams in them. Beams of a beautiful inner light. Beams of a flexible inner steel. An ineffable beaming without ground that is, for me, the essence of our shared transness—not our transfigured flesh, which is but a means to life, but rather the radiant force of the life that shines through it. I have no idea what the Tannhäuser Gate might look like, but it can't be any grander that what being trans has already shown me. I glimpse those same visions of transcendence glittering in the pages of this book.

Susan Stryker is an award-winning scholar and filmmaker whose historical research, theoretical writing, and creative works have helped shape the cultural conversation on transgender topics since the early 1990s.

PREFACE BY MORGAN M PAGE

Memoir is a problem. As Viviane Namaste pointed out almost twenty years ago, trans narratives are constrained by the "autobiographical imperative," the push by cis people to tell Our Story on Their Terms: *We always knew, we grew up as a tomboy/sissy, we got on hormones, we had the surgery*, all in a standard, linear format. For a hundred years, these medical and pulp memoir narratives—from Freud's case studies to Christine Jorgensen's autobiography to Janet Mock's *Redefining Realness*—have flooded the niche market within which our lives are held, drowning out all other, more complicated possibilities. And perhaps, because they were up to then invisible, and up to then could only ever imagine a cis audience, they had to. As Cooper writes in this collection, "Early trans memoir threw a sheet over the ghost so it could be seen."

But now that we can see the ghost, or at least the sheet, what are we to do about it? How do we animate the spirit?

What do we hear when we let the spirit sing? And what will we find when we tear the sheet off?

Pass with Care lifts the veil of simplified, standardized trans life narratives. Cooper offers us a hand up onto the back of his motorcycle as he drives us not only from Boston to San Francisco to Santa Fe to Portland, but also deep into the heart of Americana. In *Pass with Care*, Cooper turns a mirror back on masculinity, revealing himself to be, as he writes in "Man Pageant, Unscripted," on his "own private anthropological investigation."

Though some trans people may object to Cooper's careful study of the signifiers of white American masculinity—as does one exasperated commenter on one of Cooper's *Original Plumbing* pieces, who writes how they're "tired of stories about masculinity and hard times and motorcycles and gyms and blah blah blah"—Cooper goes "as a spy, undetectable as anyone other than a man who's always had the promise of facial hair on his horizon."

Manhood might be boring, as Cooper writes—though, fanning myself, I would counter that it has a deep erotic charge, a charge that tears through *Pass with Care* like desert lightning—but its unexamined and unreflexive state is what allows so much of it to stagnate, to turn toxic. Trans men, as intrepid voyagers into masculinity, are uniquely situated to chart its dark forests and jagged peaks. In this work, Cooper joins other contemporary transmasculine writers like Thomas Page McBee (*Amateur, Man Alive*), T Cooper (*Real*

Man Adventures), and Paul B. Preciado (*Testo Junkie*), whose works form the core of emerging trans men's literature that critically interrogates the construction of manhood.

What Cooper reveals is a woundedness at the heart of American masculinity. This woundedness splinters in the lives and bodies of trans men, who are forced to confront not only their own pain, but also the dissonance of seeing the problems of masculinity from its outer margins and being compelled on some level to move even further within the mouth of the beast. As Cooper writes of this sometimes unsettling awareness in "Sharing Trans," "I remembered reading an ominous anecdote written somewhere by a trans man in an FTM newsletter: 'You can choose to become a man, but you can't choose the man you will become.'"

The man we watch Cooper become in *Pass with Care*—the working-class punk, the lover of queer femmes, the rageful Buddhist—is one achingly conscious of his own implication in the gears of masculinity. One who knows that he is hurt and hurting. One who, most importantly of all, strives to undo and to do better. In one of the most moving pieces in this collection, "Splinters," Cooper writes about how his process of transition—kicking off with a short trip to New Mexico that lasts eight years—was an act of healing a wound: "I went out into the desert alone and by the light of the waning moon I pulled each splinter free."

Though he moves us through his own private anthropology across the rough terrain of masculinity, from all-welcoming beard contests in Portland to the cruel bonding of pigeon-hunting in a fabrication shop in San Francisco, throughout *Pass with Care* we hold tight to Cooper's waist on the back of his motorcycle, abandoning the straightforward linearity of time and transition that consumes so much of autobiographical work by trans people. Cooper uses his own narratives—not singular—to explore loss, invisibility, sex, and the difficult but necessary work of healing. As he writes in "Throwing a Sheet over the Ghost," "It seems like our duty as trans people writing memoir in this time is to resist and reject narrative forms and chronologies that limit the diversity of our multivalent trans bodies and lives."

Cooper might not solve all the problems troubling trans memoir, but he shows us what it sounds like when we let its spirit sing.

Morgan M Page is a writer, artist, and historian in London, England. Her podcast, One From the Vaults, *is the one and only podcast that brings all of the dirt, gossip, and glamour from trans history.*

INTRODUCTION

In 1997, I got into the van with Sister Spit and my life changed, if only for the taste it gave me of what it felt like to live as an artist twenty-four hours a day. In the van, we traveled backward, away from the golden West where we'd all run away to, back across the bleeding and foreign heartlands and belts hewn of rust and biblical verse and corn and cattle and puritanical, throbbing metropolises, the uppity older cousins that scoffed at the amorphous parameters of our West Coast mecca. We traveled back to the places that had rejected us, hurt us, shunned us, and we made peace with them. We shook off the fear that living in a paradise of your own making can begin to manufacture about the outside world. Having had the experience of feeling desire and creativity rather than fear and persecution, we'd begun to let down our guard, and we'd imagined that going back onto the battlefield was to go naked and unarmed. We received threats and insults, a promise to have our heads blown off with a shotgun in Some Dark Strip of Nowhere, Alabama.

And we were met with love and free booze and propositions in cities small and large, in places that had once turned us away or warned us not to come to begin with—in these places, we learned we weren't just welcome, we were needed.

One of the first pieces that I performed, "Lips like Elvis," overtly explored my dubious relationship to gender. More importantly, it explored how other people responded to my non-conforming gender presentation. I lived then as a very masculine butch, though I'd always wrestled with an unnamable awareness of physical dysphoria. I'd shrugged off the femaleness attributed to me as something I was stuck with, something immutable that did not compute. But upon landing into the undulating and glittering, comforting and celebrating, queer weirdo arms of San Francisco in 1993, I realized how naive I'd been. There were more genders and expressions of such than we even had language to keep up with. Our permutations variegated faster than any taxonomy could pace. I was able to live in a self-made, imperfect utopia of queer artists and writers and musicians and sex workers and activists, and here I was welcomed to inhabit my own form, to fill the sides of my retreated-from arroyos with all of the exploration and desire I could muster. No matter how bereft and lost I'd been upon arrival, San Francisco was there to quench my thirst and to make known the desires I'd lacked the imagination to conceive as possible in the past.

The community of queer artists that took me in made lots of space for us to inhabit our genders as we saw fit, but anywhere outside of that world meant I had to combat questions and shaming for not fitting expectations of gender.

On that tour, I performed my Elvis piece in a pompadour that was perhaps more Lenny and Squiggy than rockabilly, and I wrestled with what I was. My identity was questioned both inside and outside of the van. I was hauled out of women's restrooms by security guards for looking like a man, questioned at the doors of both a famous butch/femme bar in Buffalo and a dance club in my former haunt of Provincetown (it was ladies' night, after all), and kicked out of a men's leather bar for looking not enough like one. My path shimmered before me like a heat mirage on a desert highway, gone by the time I was close enough to the spot.

Writing these past twenty years played a crucial role not only in finding myself, but also in carving out a space in which to authentically exist. In the early '90s-San Francisco I found myself in, a pre-Internet world, queer literature was "published" in public performance and in scrappy zines. Copies were made via stolen and re-gifted analog counters that one would plug into the Xerox machine and then repocket. The outlets for subversive queer stories were largely limited to those we could carve out for ourselves. I was self-taught, learning to write by performing and listening to my compatriots perform. As a gender non-conforming queer artist, I got to tell the stories that my culture told me were not worth listening to for over two decades.

As I reshaped my body through rudimentary medical technology to inhabit a form that somewhat closed the gap of physical dissonance wracking my days, I found myself less and less able to find my voice on the stage. My actual voice changed, and as my vocal cords thickened and shortened, the effort it took to project my voice on stage increased. I wanted to figure out how to close the gap between how people engaged with my now-scruffy face and burly body and my swaggeringly euphoric queer writing voice. I wanted to learn how to write for the slower burn and deeper engagement of the page.

Much of my early writing about gender was a way of responding in conversation to others when I was unable to in the moment, in person. It took me a long time to name feelings, to choose the words. It felt as if language did not yet exist for what I needed to describe. I dug for it in my writing. Much of the early writing was an attempt to convince or explain my trans life to hostile others. As time passed, my own rigidity and need to name and define myself relaxed, a long-taut line gone just slack enough.

The world has changed so much over that same period of time. Increasingly, gender has become a subject of discourse and resistance in a politicized world; language has expanded and invented and innovated to allow for more and more of us to exist. For every step forward that we make as a culture, we still have to fight against retrograde ideologues who seek to control our autonomy over our own bodies.

I've changed profoundly over the last two decades, as well. And it's not possible for me to consider what it means to move through the world as a man without also reckoning my whiteness and my place in the machine of colonial capitalism. The urgency of our current moment means that for someone of my privileges it's not enough to simply question masculinity—one must also act.

Writer Max Gladstone recently Tweeted a conversation he'd had with his father. He asked, "But how are we supposed to be men in the [21st] century?"

His father replied, "Hard question. But you start by not being a fucking fascist."

As I exit my forties, the biggest transition I face is what it means to age in a trans body that never quite expected to make it out of the 1990s alive. Death and loss surrounded me as I came of age. In a culture that insisted that people like me are sick aberrations, I struggled to ever conceive of a future. But the future came, whether I was ready for it or not, and it has been so fucking beautiful: terrible, ugly, sexy, lustful, creative, delirious, heartbreaking, joyful, lonely, loving, and brilliant. I can't wait to see what happens next.

PASS WITH CARE

A Trans Body's Path in Eight Folds

"Thou wast not born for death, immortal Bird!
No hungry generations tread thee down."
–JOHN KEATS, "ODE TO A NIGHTINGALE"

One: right concentration

A trans body sightsees at Carlsbad Caverns. It pays admission and enters the gap-toothed maw. Eyes are open but not working at first, seeing only the green opposite of the hot, white outside. Soon, the trans eyes forget the world's way of seeing, in favor of its own vision in the cool balm of dark. It feels a kinship with the stalactites fanging down from the dark ribbed roof, growing and changing ever so slowly, drip by drip—an inch a century, if that. The waiting and the long unfolding to *become*, molecule by molecule. In the yellowing glow of a miner's headlamp, the trans body spelunks toward nature's confirmation of the impossible made manifest, and vows to cultivate the patience of a cave.

Two: right action

A trans body visits a lover in a high desert town in the American Southwest. While running near to panting from altitude on a community center treadmill, this trans body spots another trans body on an adjacent treadmill, two machines over. A wash of warm recognition floods the one at the sight of an other. The trans body runs in place and listens to punk rock through headphones while shaping a way to connect with the other trans body. *Hello*, it imagines saying, *me too*. Or, *I am your people*. Too stiff? Too awkward? *I am so happy you and I are here together in this place, of all places. How many more of us might be here?* Slowing the treadmill down to run, tripping on the flapping, black rubber belt, the trans body knows it cannot make any reach toward the other. More likely than a welcomed connection, it could be received as an affront, a highlighting of some failure of detail—or worse, a dangerous positioning of crosshairs on the back of the other. One trans body might go undetected, but two trans bodies begin to shape an identifiable pattern. Two trans bodies dismount treadmills, sweating, alone.

Three: right speech
A trans body meets another trans body for coffee. In the span of drinking a twelve-ounce Americano, one trans body is smudged out and rendered invisible by the other. Countless people wield the power to erase a trans body, but nothing wounds to the same extent as when it happens by the hands of another trans body. A trans body rents a place with a friend. The friend leans on the trans body sometimes, as if they were spouses, or two old trees bordering a field who fell

into each other in a windstorm—hard to tell who is holding the other up. The friend sometimes shakes out tired assumptions about "X" or "Y," like wet wash about to be pinned to a line that only extends in two finite directions. One day, the friend-spouse directs the trans body to do something in a highly divided public space. When the trans body reminds the housemate-friend why this suggested action would not be ideal, how it would expose, embarrass, or worse, imperil a trans body, the spousemate says, *Sometimes I forget you are trans*, sharp with darts of exasperation, like the trans body's transness is the most difficult thing in the world for the housemate (and friend) to bear, and yet the easiest thing in the world to forget.

Four: right view
A trans body is denoted "A" at birth, but by surviving over half a lifetime of social misadventures, zigzagging rat-maze bureaucracy, hustling the system, defying critics and nay-sayers huddled in worn camps around smoldering embers of damp fires, performing emotional sorcery, the application of rudimentary medical technology, and a highly honed ability to charm service workers and gatekeeping personnel at each level of the salt-sea lock, a trans body is able to exist in relative comfort as "B." This trans body's ability to live as "B" magnetizes to itself praise and blame in equal and alternating currents. This trans body's comfort in inhabiting "B" does not stand as a referendum on "A," nor upon A_1, A_2, A_3

. . . B1, B2 . . . nor does it deny the existence of "C." It simply feels like if it has to choose a climate—say, the sandstone, hot, dry desert or the gray-green, damp, pine woods—it chooses woods. The trans body still loves the desert for its own magic light, but a place only feels like home when it is home.

Five: right intention
A trans body telegraphs thinly coded messages over the wire. The information is everywhere, but the connections are fleeting when they are soldered together at all. Birds fly out with destinations imprinted in their minds and scrolls tied to their feet. Sometimes they land, and other times they never come home to roost, eliciting neither hope nor surprise. They do the work of gossip but are much cuter, albeit in an archaic way. The messenger birds are too troublesome for white, urban, middle-class young adults to co-opt. Far offshore, there are other trans bodies bobbing like tiny ships in dark water, their little red lights blinking out, *I'm here, I'm here, I'm here.* Within the empty shape of a few beats, a slower light arcs out from atop a rocky cliff, slicing the black water apart from the blackening sky like a cake, its beam refracted through the thick-scaled Fresnel prisms of the lighthouse lamp. In a brief whip and sweep away, it answers back, *Alone, alone*—blink, sweep—*alone, alone.* On land, the fallen are called bodies, but at sea, the lost are called souls.

Six: right effort

A trans body goes to the low-cost clinic on indigent status and performs a show. The most complex and personal interstices of self and body are reduced to carved, primary-colored wooden blocks and ABCs. The trans body has been trans longer than the doctor has been a doctor. The teacher pretends to be a student. The trans body is a bad kid in school who says what you want to hear to avoid detention. This trans body trains the doctor to see it as a patient and its needs as deserving of care, much in the same way wolves once trained humans to see them as dogs.

Seven: right livelihood

A trans body lives and dies a young trans life within the cold, blue frame of a screen. Another trans body takes shape in the late afternoon of midlife, confounding those around in concentric ripples that dissipate with distance. Ejected and unwanted, as burnt as toast from the chrome slots of society, a trans body walks a rain-soaked alley bearing a heavy bindlestiff as an exhausting punishment for noncompliance. One trans body bikes the bridge and stops at the midpoint to stare at the river below and listen for the call of sirens, while another trans body's fist connects with the jaw of a would-be attacker. Another trans body jostles past on a downtown sidewalk, unnoticed, while another stands at a podium, grasping a bronze trophy of recognition. A trans body cradles a child in tender arms. Despair and hope pulse through a trans body in equal measure. Beneath flesh, the bones of the trans body are as likely as the non-trans body to receive the frequency of either vibration. Only the path of sound differs.

Eight: right mindfulness

The trans body asks for something so internal and deeply known to be named, something that longs for a witness in the clean light of day. The trans body asks for an expansion of what is perceived to be conceivable, to be included in the taxonomy of the "real." The human mind often discovers that what we thought to be one thing is indeed another, and that new knowledge is embraced with joy—Pluto is not a planet, we are a galaxy among countless others, we can listen to the sound of a comet streaking a fiery brushstroke across the silence of space, we can measure the code of our DNA against the matrix of the trees. Human hearts and imaginations swell at what is possible. A trans body asks that the wonder of the world *contains it* within all of the world's resplendent glory.

Lincoln Street

Uncle Neil makes a bike for me. I don't know what the occasion is, but one day, there it is, the best bicycle you've ever seen. The long banana seat and tasseled hand grips are shiny, shiny red. It has small wheels and chopper handlebars and a tall loop of a sissy bar, all chrome. It has fixed gears and back-pedal brakes, and a chain guard that rattles at high speeds.

Uncle Neil—he's really my great-uncle, my grandfather's brother-in-law—is a little guy, trim and dapper in a plaid shirt tucked into dark Levi's, pointy cowboy boots, black hair combed back with Brylcreem, face tan and wrinkled, the etched lines polished smooth like driftwood, a turquoise and silver ring on his pinky finger, a hint of whiskey behind the prevalent smoky smell. The basement of his and Aunt Bev's house is a dim, musty workshop, and it's here that the best bike of my life is built from spare parts. He puts the two-wheeled Frankenstein's monster together and paints it with flat spray paint, some of it Easter-dress yellow, some of it robin's egg blue.

There are people around, but I spend a lot of time alone, reading books out in my fort. And when I'm not, I'm riding that bike, the one Uncle Neil made for me. My great-grandmother lives right next door in that white house, and next to her lives Grandma Jeanne and Uncle John, Uncle Ed, Aunt Helen, Aunt Joan, Uncle Larry, Aunt Patty, Aunt Cecelia, and Aunt Mary. Cecelia is three years older than me, and we all call her "Cie." Mary, my dad's youngest sister, is a year older than me.

We play "gas station" in their driveway—Mary, Cie, and me. Cie, the attendant, works at the gas station, using the garden hose to fill us up. My name is "John Wolf."

"You're *always* John Wolf," Mary says.

I use clothespins to attach baseball cards to my spokes, which makes my bike sound exactly like a motorcycle. I cruise into the driveway and shout, "Cie, fill 'er up!" Sometimes we roll up the garage door and use it as a service area, put air in our tires, use a skateboard to roll underneath Grandma Jeanne's station wagon on our backs.

At the end of the driveway are two important trees. One is a giant pine tree. In the winter, when the long boughs of the pine tree hang heavy and white, we build a circular wall of snow around the perimeter of the branches and instigate vicious snowball fights from behind the fortress.

The other important tree is the peach tree, only a few feet

away from the edge of Lincoln Street, the street I live on. In the summer, the peach tree drops countless sour, hard little fruit on the ground—never any sweet peaches, not even one. On hot summer days, long days when it feels like an entire lifetime between the time you get up and lunchtime, Mary and I sometimes sit beneath the peach tree carving faces into the unripe fruit with my jackknife and roll them across Lincoln Street. We call this game "rolling heads." Sometimes we give the carved heads names, sometimes fictitious, sometimes somebody who bugs us, like Earl Stoneham, the kid across the street my brother's age who stutters. We cheer when a car runs over one of the rolling heads in the street.

"Stay in the driveway," my mother says. Lincoln Street is a death trap. We know this. It is a long, straight street that people drive down as fast as possible. We've had three dogs and four cats get creamed on that road. First, my German Shepherd, Rusty. He ran right out into the street and was instantly killed. We got another German Shepherd; I named her Rusty also. One day Rusty II got loose and ran into the street. She was struck by a car in front of Grandma Jeanne's house and was killed. Mary and I overheard my father telling Uncle Larry about it, saying her eyeball was knocked right out of her head. Mary and I wander around by the peach tree, looking for Rusty II's eyeball amongst the semi-rotted fruit on the ground. We look for a couple of days, but never find it. We don't feel like playing "rolling heads" after that.

"No more dogs," my father says.

"Stay out of that damned street," my mother says.

And yet. The best thing in the world is to ride my bicycle up Lincoln Street, up the hill past the woods and the water towers, up past Joey Moore's house and Tammy Sanderson's house—Tammy, who called me G.I. Joe at school in front of everyone because she saw me and Cie wearing my father's army fatigues out into the woods playing "war"—all the way to where Lincoln Street meets Hancock Street. Turn around the concrete divider with the bent stop sign from a drunk driver, turn around it fast like your bike is a barrel-racing pony. Then, pedal as fast as you can back past Sarah Krake's house, Tammy Sanderson's, Joey Moore's, harder and harder as you approach the water towers—then, hunch down low to the frame, your face nearly touching the handlebars, the chain guard rattling furiously, wind through your hair like a mermaid's fingers, Lincoln Street pulling away underneath you like a satin ribbon, stomach riding somewhere up in your chest—

It's freedom, like being a bird, or something better than a person. It's fast, like being motion, rather than quiet and still. It's like you can keep going right back down Lincoln Street, past the library, and zoom off the end of it into the air like Evel Knievel over a million American flag-painted barrels, and just keep going in the sky—frozen in a glorious moment, but flying, free, away from the plainness, the stillness, the regular broken up only by dogs' deaths and drunken crashes into signposts.

ONE DAY, I think I'm alone. Nobody around at all. I'm riding back and forth on Lincoln Street, the baseball cards snapping a tinny roar through my bicycle spokes. I am alone and there's a song in my head. My arms dangle at my sides, no hands. There's a song in my head, repeating itself, begging for release. I turn around. The card-snapping slows as I change direction, needing one hand on the handlebars as I do this. I speed up, and the snapping of the baseball cards pounds a rhythm that matches the relentless song that longs to live outside of my skull:

"One banana, two banana, three banana four, four bananas make a bunch and so do many more!"

Softly to myself at first, and then it's just the best feeling, cruising along past the O'Hanrahan's house, spots of tree-shade cool from the glare of the summer sun. Summer is long and I spend most of it alone. Everyone is too busy to play, and even if they're not, I'm not always sure how it all works. Sometimes I look forward to school starting, just to be around people in a way I understand. Not because we're all friends. It's okay, even if we're together only because we have to be. But right now, it doesn't matter being alone, because I got my bike and I'm singing this song. It feels so good:

"One banana, two banana, three banana, four, four bananas make a bunch and so do many more, over hills and highways the banana buggies roll—"

Suddenly, there's movement closing up fast behind me,

a ching-chang of rusty gears shifting and a voice smeared with hatred. Both hands grip the handlebars. I slow down as I'm jolted from my dreaming and singing, and Jim DeBona overtakes me on his Huffy ten-speed, with the handlebars bent backwards the tall way. His freckles are 3-D on his pale face, his eyes dark, narrow, and mean.

"Wuuun bananaaah, twooo bananaaah, threeee banana-nahhh, foooour!" he sneers at me, then he rides away laughing, shirtless, his Huffy creaking and complaining.

"Shut up, Boner," I yell, but he's already gone. I try to sing again, but my song feels stupid. Even riding my bike feels stupid. I look around, feeling like the entire street is watching me get busted by Jimmy DeBona. Everyone calls him "The Boner," and I used to think it was because he was so skinny you could see all of his bones, or because, you know, his name. Nobody's around as I scan up the street. Nobody except Maisie Woodsman's littlest sister, who always stands out on their front stairs buck naked, witnesses my humiliation. It doesn't even matter that he's *the* biggest loser. I shuffle home and put my bike under the porch.

Cie and I sit in the front seat of Grandma Jeanne's brown station wagon with the fake wooden sides, parked in the driveway by the basketball hoop. "They call him 'The Boner' because he's a fucking dick," Cie says, "not because he's bony."

Cie never calls me dense or anything, but sometimes I just feel like it when she talks. She knows everything. Once she drew a uterus and fallopian tubes in the dirt with a stick and explained periods and pregnancy to me. Cie got the Foreigner 4 album before anyone else and we listened to it in the pop-up camper, full-blast.

Cie pushes in the lighter as we sit with our feet up on the dashboard. When it pops out, she presses the end of a pine needle into the glowing metal, until pungent smoke wafts through the car—good, but kind of sickening.

"Do you know what 69 is?" Cie asks.

Not wanting to say no, I shrug.

She quickly pulls off her black Converse low-tops.

"This is the boy," she says, hefting up the sneaker in her left hand, "and this is the girl." She nods to the sneaker in her right hand. "And the toes are their faces!"

She inverts one sneaker, so the toe faces down, and mashes them together. I just look, and don't say anything. A picture flickers through my head of Jimmy DeBona's face against my crotch and my face pressed into the coarse Toughskin jeans he always wears, even in the worst heat of summer.

"Gross," I say.

"You'll figure it all out soon enough," Cie says. "Do you like any boys yet?"

"No," I say. I slip out of the car and run into Grandma Jeanne's backyard, and in two fast strides I climb to the top of the big granite rock. I stand there, feeling tall. I put my arms all the way up, making myself taller. The sun's going down, and a coolness moves across the yard like an exhale of relief. The cricket symphony begins, echoed by the bullfrogs in the swamp across Lincoln Street. Dad pulls up, home from work.

It doesn't matter that I don't know what 69 is, or periods, or that I don't like any boy. I know everything else. I know how to play poker, and I know four magic tricks with cards. I have a jackknife and a toolbox. I know how to build a teepee and I know the call of the chickadee. I know how to plant things in Dad's garden, and I know how to stain wood. I know how to draw pictures and ride horses. I know how to worm a hook and clean the fish I catch. I have a new dog named Lucky, and he is all mine. He knows how to stay out of the street and likes to play rodeo with me. He waits for me when I get home from school. I have a red, yellow, and blue bicycle, and I know how to make freedom.

Boombox

I took one look at my new boombox and I knew then and there that I would never be cool. The boombox was my parents' gift to me for my twelfth birthday, and as the weather warmed from algid, damp spring to the humid murmurings of early summer in the South Shore of Boston, I made tentative forays out into my neighborhood with my boombox as company.

The small, chrome, Panasonic boombox was all of a foot long. It had an AM/FM radio tuner along the top and a round, silver knob set in the center. To the left of the radio dial lived a single, round speaker. The right side of the tiny boombox housed a rectangular, marsupial flap in which to insert 8-track tapes. When I opened the boombox birthday gift, I understood on an intrinsic, nonverbal frequency that it precluded any chance of me being perceived as a cool kid. The kids who smoked cigarettes behind Cumby's, where their cool older siblings had long ago spray-painted the word "YES" in a bubble-letter salute to that band and sold baggies of three jays for a five-spot. The kids who wrote O-Z-Z-Y across the knuckles of their left hands in ballpoint and who blasted hard rock out of their normal boomboxes—the ones with two speakers and cassette-tape players. Or the kids—the rare pioneers—who listened to percussive beats of early hip-hop and practiced their back-spins on a piece of cardboard . . . no, my categorization as something that hovered outside the perimeters of cool was now cemented and unmovable. I saw that rectangle hole for 8-track cassette tapes, and my future hopes for any scrap of coolness fell into it. The asymmetry, imbalance, and awkward, heavy construction of the chrome and black boombox mirrored back a self-portrait in electronics form.

All of the elements of my family dynamics—as I could best comprehend at age twelve—were also framed within the boombox's clunky chrome rectangle. Our young family's struggles and aspirations made loud drop-shifts forward from working-class to middle like the track changes on the 8-track tapes. My parents were thirty-four years old, with three children between the ages of one and twelve. Mom cut hair at home at our kitchen table, with Donahue yapping from a small TV on the counter. A micro-climate of hair bleach and Aqua Net hovered over the house on days she worked. If she was doing her own mother's weekly hairdo, the forbidden stench of cigarette smoke cloyed the air as well.

My dad, the oldest of nine children, was a college student when I was born, and now was well into his career as a civil engineer and a captain in the Army Corps of Engineers. I was the oldest child of two eldest children, who were raised to not complain, to not expect much, and to not feel entitled to anything you didn't personally work your ass off for. The new one-speaker, 8-track radio was a physical manifestation of how hard my parents worked to give me something they thought that I wanted. Though it wasn't quite right, it was an offering, and I knew even then that I could not complain or ask for a different thing than what I'd been given. It was better to be grateful than to get exactly what you wanted.

My gratitude was genuine, and it plummeted down as deep as my disappointment. In that depth, I felt a soft bruise of sorrow for something I could not name. I heard the arrows of my parents' attempts at love whiz past my head, the shots never quite sticking the mark of my heart, but the efforts were palpable, nonetheless. None of us knew what we were doing, but we were all giving it our best. My chest swelled with an amplitude of chagrin at my own disappointment, and in that gap between the gratitude and shame flourished the wow and flutter of feeling unseen.

It was 1981, and I was a tall, awkward pork chop of a girl in boys' clothes, with a thicket of dark hair that hugged my round face like an over-padded helmet. I wore ratty cut-offs that my mother threatened to destroy if I ever took them off, white tube socks with three stripes—red, blue, and red—that clamped the top curves of my calves, and a worn-thin, Kelly-green T-shirt that just hugged the tender protrusions that had begun to emerge on my chest, much to my utter, unspeakable dismay. I also wore a red and white Peterbilt trucker hat backwards on my head, smashed down over the mass of my burnt-umber hair, causing the ends of my would-be Dorothy Hamill haircut to bozo out at the sides.

The hat was a gift from my long-haul driving grandpa, who came back from trucking runs to the southern United States with forbidden delights, like illegal fireworks. My younger brother, Chris, and I wrested the hat back and forth from each other over the years, and during the summer of age twelve the Peterbilt hat was a red, proud crown I sported on the very precipice of discovering that the way I felt most comfortable in my clothes—and in my body—was about to be a massive source of concern, heckling, intervention, embarrassment, and shame. I had no idea what was to come.

I walked through empty neighborhood streets and the dirt paths in the woods surrounding us. I hefted the asymmetric boombox to my right shoulder and played one of my five 8-track tapes on repeat, the tapes too bulky to carry extras with me in a cut-off jeans pocket. High notes rattled a thin timbre on the perforated metal circle of the lone speaker. Sometimes it was Fleetwood Mac's *Rumours* that I inserted into the boombox, with its peeling label image of Mick Fleetwood's disturbing ren-faire tights and—what the hell were those dangling, jangling silver orbs that hung from strings below his crotch, directly in the sight line of Stevie's diaphanous, downward twirl? What was the *stuff* one was let to do, once they were laid-me-down in the tall grass? Both curious and terrified, I could only wonder.

But I didn't have to wonder too hard. After years of careful study of my father's porn collection, I had some idea. What happened in the tall grass was vague and conceptual, an idea that reverberated along the springboard of my body, though I didn't understand the trajectory or the subsequent plunge. I studied those magazines carefully, and the only certain answer I came up with after looking at page after page of women's sepia curves, pendulous breasts, and cheerful bushes, aside from a pang of undefined desire, was, *Not me, not me, not me.*

A year later, I will acquiesce to the clammy hands of my friend Desiree's fourteen-year-old brother and trade him access to my body for a shot at success as a girl. In the woods, my knees in damp pine-needles, he will push at me with his tiny pink erection, which will evoke in my mind images of newborn mice and sausages from metal tins and I will say "mmhmm," when he asks if it feels good. *At least he will ask.* Later, I will find neither my desire satisfied nor my attempt to be a normal girl anointed by his baby mouse cock. Another failure on record: the thirteen-year-old girl who looks like a boy and gives it up in the woods. I will punch him in his stomach for telling everyone at school that I kiss like a dog.

But now, in the summer of 1981, I listened to the crunch and twang of the *Southern Fried Rock* compilation, or the orchestral *Star Wars* movie soundtrack, or Bob Seger's *Against the Wind*, with its stampede of wild horses on the label, or else his *Live Bullet* album with the pulsing magenta, stage-light blur of Bob Seger and his hair. Lost in the music, sometimes I'd forget about my dread of any neighborhood kid spotting me with the boombox. Other times, I'd roll a movie in my imagination about a kid giving me a bunch of shit about my lame nerd boombox and I would picture myself strong and powerful enough to stand up for myself, defending the merits of my boombox—*hey pal, better than no boombox at all*. Or, best of all, I'd imagine myself unaffected, immune to the taunts and opinions of my peers, above it all, buoyed by the words of .38 Special: "Hold on loosely, hold on loosely."

I'd find a warm dry bed of pine needles in the woods and lie back, watching the clouds skip past the jagged openings of the high tree canopy, my arm tucked behind my shaggy head for a pillow and a long stem of grass sweet and pungent between my teeth. I'd sing along with Seger's *Live Bullet*. I found the use of saxophone in '80s music to be a cheesy affront to my ears, but in the opening notes of "Turn the Page," the sax took on something of a Hank Williams, high-lonesome whine. A stanza in the middle of the song mesmerized me:

"Well, you walk into a restaurant strung out from the road
And you feel the eyes upon you as you're shaking off the cold
You pretend it doesn't bother you, but you just want to
    explode
Most times you can't hear 'em talk, other times you can
All the same old clichés, is that a woman or a man?
You always seem outnumbered, so you don't dare make a
    stand . . ."

It would be another ten years before I knew firsthand the feeling of coming off the road and into the Klieg-light glare of those eyes Bob Seger was talking about. But even then, while I didn't completely understand all of the variegations of gender or conformity in the song, I still knew that it had something to do with me—the way that I always cast an awkward shape trying to fit into a smaller space, described and prescribed for me by the words and looks and comments and admonishments of everyone around me.

It seeped into me by osmosis, from the atmosphere itself. I was a block of wet clay being quietly punched into a shape I didn't want to take by the people around me, even those who purported to love me. It would be another ten years before I understood what it felt like to be strung out from the road, but right then, at age twelve, in the woods with my uncool boombox and my thick, straight body and my tube socks and my trucker hat, I sang along with my 8-tracks and I knew, somehow, that being myself would entail a long, rough swim upriver, and that I would have to fight to keep the shape of myself intact. I knew that it would hurt me, and that it would be lonely, and that I probably would never be cool or popular. I listened to Bob Seger singing about being young and strong, or even older now, but still running, running against the wind, and I knew that I could forge the quiet solidity of myself into an intactness that no one could ever steal.

Prayer for the Workingman

Sometimes it is the smallest things that surprise you. The kindness of a teamster, for instance. The hammers are already falling by the time my fog fades, but it is early enough, anyway. Roach coaches pace their street corners as possessively as dealers; broad-shouldered men with hard hats and thermoses tucked under their arms wander away slowly from the 22-line bus stop. Pigeons and seagulls flap silently between dumpsters, gathering breakfast while most of the city still sleeps.

I think my motorcycle, it knows the way, like that horse in the Robert Frost poem. It carries me to work without me even thinking about it, without so much as a little nudge in its ribs. Next thing you know, I'm at the top of Potrero Hill and the sun scrambles its way on top of Oakland, the container cranes like prehistoric beasts in the surly dawn light. Lucky for me, my baby likes my Carhartt's dirty and my palms callused, because I'll tell you, when dusk falls and I'm done shouldering my corner of the American dream for another day, I sure as fuck don't feel like a poor man's Paul Newman. Some Casanova with a weary spine. Some days, it's easier to drink the ache out than it is to push it through the gristmill and hope it oozes out the other end as art.

What you trade for a steady paycheck and worker's pride is the dullness that lack of surprise gives you. Good for the soul, bad for the back, or vice versa. A little security, a little hard work, and a card to punch every day squeezes the spontaneity out from every pore. Sometimes the good, slow, and steady life puts a bullet in creativity. You need those broken-open, broken-through moments to step back and see and regurgitate your findings as poetry.

Peace won't be had in this exchange. When art lives inside of you like a parasitic conjoined twin who longs for a life of its own, you won't quell those urges by plunging into labor. Maybe Walt Whitman could do it, but these are different days. It's hard enough to have art, even while you're making it. All you really get when you embark upon work you do not truly love, is knowing that every next day will mirror the last until your back gives out, your knees give out, or your meter expires. Hopefully by then you'll have squirreled away enough cash for a mortgage, your kid's college education, or that brand-new, full-size Ford pick-up truck you've yearned for for years.

One thing I've learned watching my father bust his ass his whole life is that the dream of *things* is not my dream. I build my family and fortress in intangible brick-and-mortar of experience. I imagine that I am carrying on the work of my grandfathers, one the forklift driver and union shop steward at a soap factory and the other a long-haul truck driver. The myth of bootstraps is nailed to my psyche. I'm the bastard amalgamation of capability, working-class pride, and queerness. There is so little time to do the work that fixes the world when you are working in the trades. There is so little time to make the art that reflects the world back upon itself so that it can know itself in time.

Blessed are they who can swing a hammer in one hand and a paintbrush in the other. Blessed are they who smooth concrete with one hand and comfort a child or a grandparent or a lonely, lost, or homeless soul with the other. Blessed are they who reach across. Blessed are they who hold up the voices of the unheard and poor and suffering and many.

Identity Poem

A Man Trapped in a Woman's Body.

A Drag Queen Trapped in a Bulldagger's Body.

A Heterosexual White Man Trapped in a Drag Queen's Body, Which Is Trapped in a Butch Dyke's Body. A Cross-Dressing Straight Man Trapped in a Bear Fag's Body That Is Trapped in a Female-To-Male Transsexual's Body That Is Trapped in the Body of a Once-Heterosexual-but-Now-Gay Woman.

A Male-Identified Straight Womyn-With-A-Y-Born-Woman Trapped in the Body of a Lesbian Male-To-Female Transgender Woman's Body. A Soccer Mom Trapped in a Leatherdaddy's Body. A Dog Trapped in a Human Body. A Trans-Species Cat-To-Dog Trapped in the Body of a Bisexual Man Trapped in the Body of a Fifth Grader from Suburban Massachusetts. A Swimmer Trapped in a Shark's Body. A Body Trapped in an Idea of a Body.

The Conversation

One

Is it your tits? Why don't you just get your tits cut off and be a dyke? You always were my lumberjack guy. I just think it's much more radical to walk the line in-between. I like the contradiction between your gender and your body. You know I love you, Cooper, but I don't know why you'd want to be a man—I just don't like men!

All butches are gender-dysphoric!

What's wrong with being a butch? What's wrong with being a dyke? Why would you want to cut up your body like that?

You are the perfect man for me, Cooper Lee.

I don't understand what makes you so different from all the butches I've slept with.

I think you're the butchest person I've ever slept with.

You are a real man. Are we the third sex, Cooper? I'm just afraid you won't want to do dyke things anymore. Don't be afraid to confront the boss—you're more of a man than he is! It's just your internalized misogyny. I'm afraid we won't be read as queer anymore—I mean, I'm a *dyke!* I like butches who are *into* their tits! All of the butches are becoming men. Who am I going to date *now*?

Do you prefer "he" or "she"?

Look at him. He's the poster child for why you *shouldn't* take testosterone. Maybe more trans women would perform at your show if there was more lip-synching.

I am *way* manlier than most of the trans men that I have met. The trans movement is all white. You hate your body. You're copping out on the queers.

I won't call you *he* because I think politically you should stay "in-between;" besides, I don't see what makes you such a *guy*!

Hey, are you gonna get a phalloplasty? You'd be surprised by what people like me have learned about people like *you* by watching cable TV health shows.

When people at work call you "she," I'm like *dude, what the fuck!* It's so weird. I mean, it just makes sense to call you "he."

I just think that if you can find some way to be happy in the body you have, you should try to do that. It just seems like a really hard life to be a transsexual.

I love the person you are in the world.

If that's what you decide to do, I can go through that with you.

I'm excited to see you be more comfortable.

Someone asked me if I had a big brother named Cooper in San Francisco—I said, "*Hell, yeah!*"

You were the first of my friends to come out as trans—I owe you an apology for being so ignorant.

I will love you no matter what.

Two

Before I knew I was a human being and *not* a dog, my earliest sense of myself was male. I am just a funny sort of guy. I don't hate my female body, I just don't recognize it as mine.

I wouldn't trade the path of my life for anything. I'm glad I was raised female.

I don't even like to take Advil. I don't like the idea of needing the permission of a doctor or shrink to get what I want. Haven't they invented "Boobs-Away" cream yet? It isn't about "becoming" another person—I already am who I am—I just want my body to reflect that.

It's not like I'm suddenly changing from the person you've always known—this is more about your willingness to see who I've always been.

You don't have to understand. You just have to believe me.

I didn't know the dyke nation could be so easily shaken.

I am afraid of losing my community. I've done a lot for this community. What difference does it make how I identify?

I think it's far more radical to proudly say who you are and be vocal about it than to be invisible out of fear of rejection. It's not my responsibility to keep the world of dykes sacrosanct.

This will kill my parents. I wonder if I'll get fired.

I'm not sure which is worse: feeling invisible as trans when being perceived as a butch dyke, or feeling invisible as a queer when being perceived as a man. There's nothing wrong with being a butch, except for the fact that I am not a woman.

I have never been a woman having sex with another woman.

I wish your internalized sexism/classism/racism didn't keep you from *seeing* trans people. Just because the two trans guys you happen to know in this small community are white doesn't mean all trans guys are white.

The older I get, the harder it is to reconcile the discrepancy between my body and my mind.

My gender has always been consistent—okay, except for that very brief stint in high school where I tried really, really hard to look like a girl and failed horribly. My gender has always been this. I was dressing like this back when you were wearing pumps to work.

Dude, if doctors could surgically create a working penis, don't you think *you* would get one, dude?

I wish people got as excited about all of the differences between each other as much as they get excited about all of the different kinds of dogs at the park.

No, *I'm* the boyfriend.

I'm your man. I'm the porridge Goldilocks picked—*just right*. "He" just feels truer. I think of myself as this dude, but around the guys at work I realize I'm not one of them, either.

Nobody passes in San Francisco.

Every day, we must learn again how to love ourselves. I wonder what it feels like to be at home in your body. It's nice of you to promise to stay, but people hardly ever do. I have been on the outside my whole life; I am not afraid of being outside.

If people are going to view me as a straight, white man, it is my responsibility to live as the best man I can be.

I don't want to disappear into the world as a straight man.

I don't want to disappear into the world.

I don't want to disappear.

Lips like Elvis

I first performed this piece in 1997, at an event called Trans-Central at The Lab in the Mission, San Francisco. This three-day installation and series of events was curated by artist and impresario Jordy Jones.[1] Jack Halberstam read his academic work, and gender-expansive pioneers who'd already long been cutting fresh trails through the thicket of the gender binary, like Hans Scheirl, Del LaGrace Volcano, Rodney O'Neal Austin, and Justin Vivian Bond, were among the artists and performers involved. I was the new kid, scared and doe-eyed, wondering if I belonged there at all, wondering if the word "trans" was strong enough to hold me, or if I was strong enough to be held by it.

A few months later I performed "Lips like Elvis" at the International Foundation for Gender Education (IFGE) Conference's "Masculinities Program," aboard the Queen Mary in Long Beach, CA on April 18, 1997. It was for a panel called "When the Bow Breaks: Masculinities and Genderqueerness in the Arts," which was organized by Danielle Abrams and also featured Jamison Green and the photography of Loren Cameron, who had made transmasculine people and bodies visibly beautiful in a way they'd never been prior. Other presenters in the Masculinities Program included trailblazing FTM artists and scholars such as Spencer Bergstedt, Jason Cromwell, Jordy Jones, Guy Baldwin, Jacob Hale, and Jude Patton—my elders, my ancestors. As in my moment on the stage at TransCentral, I had the sense of entering a preexisting conversation, something people long before me struggled to make real. I was among my forefathers and foremothers, artists who'd been carving out a space for years so that people like me could imagine existing. It was, and sometimes still is, so easy to think that all of these struggles, conversations, and experiences are completely new and to be borne by each of us alone, as individuals. This is white supremacist neoliberal capitalism doing its job; the more we think we are alone and striking out on our own, the first or only of our kind, the more vulnerable we are to the idea that we have not always existed and been part of the fabric of humanity.

The IFGE program description for my work says: "Bombardier will be performing a spoken word piece; a rant about love, life, polyester, being likened to the King, blurry gender, hair pomade, and the lure of power and the frailty of fame." My performance was accompanied by slides of my paintings, along with images of me taken by San Francisco photographer Farika Joyce and international photographer Del LaGrace Volcano. I remember feeling both terrified and excited. I remember the quizzical glances I received from the trans women running the registration table, and the questioning looks my rather tall girlfriend-at-the-time *garnered. I knew that look well:* Who are you, and are you one of us? *The IFGE was the only transgender organization in the world at that time to have a paid employee; they published the magazine* Transgender Tapestry. *It was largely an organization that served trans women and feminine cross-dressers—a reminder that within my own lifetime, trans men were once a barely visible population.*

I later took this piece on the road with Sister Spit's first tour around the United States in 1997, where we performed around the country, traveled by van, and slept on the living room floors of strangers for six weeks. An excerpt of "Lips like Elvis" was published in Plasm Magazine, *Issue #16, 1997. It was self-published in my zine,* Ramblin' Man, *in 1998, a zine that I printed through illicit copying and Kinkos hookups and sold on the road at Sister Spit shows. This piece, like most of my writing from this period, was created to be spoken, to be performed. It was written for the sound of it. I still love this piece for how very far away it seems from anything that I would write about my trans body now, and I still love it for the sincerity and perhaps naivete of what it set out to accomplish.*

***

She said I have lips like Elvis, running her fingers across them, smooth and warm, my cock hard and still, still inside her.

"Thang yeew, thang yew vury much," I sneer, and she

takes my bottom lip in between hers, disappears it, then bites it hard.

Treat me like a fool, treat me mean and cruel, but love me.

SHE, MY LOVER, my beautiful one, my angelic slut, my love, my sweet, sweaty fuck—she makes me look at furniture with her. In a Castro Street store, the shopkeeper looks up at me and stares. "I thought you were a guy when you first came in," he says, as I move between precariously placed armoires.

"That happens," I say.

"Yeah—" he says louder, feeling encouraged, "—I thought you were a guy when you came in. You look kinda like Elvis." If he stares at me any harder, he will be able to determine my social security number and exact weight at birth.

And then: "Is that what you were *trying* to do? *Trying* to make people think you are a guy?" Irritation gums up his words.

I am beginning to find all of the furniture in this dusty store ugly and overpriced. I look for my lover, for the door. "No," I say, "I'm not trying to make people think anything. I'm just trying to feel as much like myself as I can."

A MANAGER at work talks to me about my benefits. She explains my dental insurance and deciphers Kaiser; she is a healthcare Rosetta Stone. "It doesn't cover tattoo removal, unless it's a gang tattoo, and it doesn't cover prosthetic limbs."

She pushes a thick packet of paperwork in my direction and says, "By the way, you look like Elvis. Hollywood Elvis, not Vegas Elvis."

THIS IS a land of dreams. You could be a cowboy, an astronaut, a mystic poet, a pyrotechnician, a thief. You could be a boy, a girl, a sparkling chimera, a shining mermaid, a nelly bulldagger, or a swaggering queen. You could step out of the body you were born in like yesterday's clothes and become a butterfly—fuck the cocoon. This is a land of dreams, after all. You could be flat-chested, pompadoured, and mustachioed; resplendent with *whatever* is in your boxer briefs and sideburns and be quite content with that, freaky man. Look what the land of dreams has done to you—distortion or clarity, depending on where you hit that bend in the fun house mirror.

This is a land of wooden nickels and old-growth redwoods, beer and coffee, sex and then some. Who's to say? You can adorn yourself in the most polyester humanly possible, stand close to open flame, and still live. You can have the sunglasses and the hair and the shoes and still have never felt the heat of Memphis.

Perhaps I felt it secondhand, the heat of Memphis, still warm in the skin of a girlfriend who was born there. "Where I'm from, you don't even go out to the mailbox unless you're all done up," she once said.

IT WAS fun being the front man for a band. My friend Michelle was the drummer and she told me I could do it, so I did it, someone else believing in me almost as good as believing in myself. All my life I figured I would one day be famous, and being a singer was like tasting it, stealing a little lick of it, copping a feel of fame without needing to go to third base.

One gig, I showed up wearing a thrifted polyester leisure suit. Being the singer and all, I had no equipment to dick around with while everyone else tuned their instruments, and when someone shouted down from the crowded back stairs, "Sing Elvis!" I obliged.

"Tah-reet me like a fooool, treat me mean and croool, bu-uut love me, bu-reak muh faithful heart, tear it all uhpaaaart, but love me . . . "

The next day, someone told my mates that they liked the fact that our band had an Elvis impersonator for a singer. It was the beginning of the end for me as a front man of a group with post-Riot Grrrl aspirations.

SEE, I NEVER even liked Elvis. When I was a kid, my cousin Gail had her whole room decorated with Elvis' face, even a ceramic bust. She was an adult! When Elvis died, she cried hysterically in her room for days, Aunt Ruth called my mom and told her so. *Big deal*, I thought. *Cousin Gail doesn't even know that guy*. I had a memory of seeing Elvis punch out a nun on the Saturday afternoon movie that came on after

Creature Double Feature. Not that I had much religion or any-thing, but the idea of punching out a woman who was spend-ing her whole life trying to be so good bothered me. I was so young that I don't know if this memory is accurate, or if I just keep remembering the memory. Anyhow, I came away with the feeling that Elvis sucked.

It wasn't until I met my lover that I began to understand the cult of personality surrounding the King like urban smog. She once punched out a guy in a redneck bar for mak-ing fun of the velvet Elvis tapestry she was wearing as a skirt, which made me have a huge crush on her.

I NEVER imagined that slopping a handful of Royal Crown into my hair could ever bring anyone to compare me to the king, the legend—but this is a land of dreams, where the dead-young lead more exciting lives than if they had actually lived. How we love the collective romance of *almost* and *too soon*. This is where the great American Dream of wasting gas and owning too much stuff is manufactured and fulfilled, of wrapping your car around a tree or driving your motorcycle off a cliff, of experiencing your last moments from the per-spective of cool bathroom tile.

It's a land of lust and excess, where you can have it all and still feel empty and wonder if only the poor have ideals and virtue. Desire is stitched into leopard print and sequins, triple-knit polyester and leather. Everyone is a rock star here; everyone is in purgatory and having a blast. The wrist wounds are gone, stomachs are pumped, shards of glass are no longer embedded in faces.

This is a land of dreams, where the littlest nobody can rise forth, cover the world with their body, their face, bump their crotch against it a couple of times, and then disappear into the universe forever—cold, silent, buoyant, and black.

"YOU HAVE lips like Elvis," she says, sucking on them. This is not a dream.

Note

1. T. Benjamin Singer, "Trans Art in the 1990s: A 2001 Interview with Jordy Jones," *TSQ: Transgender Studies Quarterly* 1, no. 4 (2014): 620–626.

In This Dungeon, All Prisoners Are Free to Leave

There/Then

It was in 1998 that I first saw Zee Knuckles in a dank yet magically festive basement. We were performing, me and the crew of rowdy dyke spoken-word and performance artists I was on tour with. I thought of the Olympia queers of that time as busy little beavers, ripe with invention, turning dumpster finds and damp cellars into glorious performance spaces—at least until the cops came.

Lola was our host. A tall, curvaceous, femme cellist who belted out original songs, Lola took queerness to the next level. While we artists from San Francisco were busy being ironic and post-queer, Lola was sincere, political, and full of heart. Back in our city, we watched our favorite bands standing stock-still, arms folded across our vintage, classic rock T-shirts, cool as glaciers. Lola exploded this cynical apathy. Every time she drew that bow across the throaty strings of her cello, my gizzard tightened. I fought back tears when she sang.

The morning after our show, over greasy breakfast at the Spar Café, I was formally introduced to Lola's roommate, Zee, a trans boy slouching sulkily in a hardwood booth with headphones on, ignoring us all. He performed his sullen pout with lusciously plump lips. Despite the shaved head, dingy hoodie, and everything rumored about him—top surgery, hormones—Zee was *pretty*.

We all bought cigarettes from the tobacco counter at Spar's, because you could, and who doesn't love the romance of an ancient, dark wood café with pictures of lumberjacks and a tobacco counter to boot? I was trying to quit. *Maybe after tour.* I splurged on a pack of Export As and Zee mumbled to ask if he could bum one off me.

Zee and Lola squeezed into the van to join us for our university show in Seattle. I always liked college shows. Not only did we always receive an enthusiastic welcome, but I felt elevated in intellectual stature, even if the potential existed for students' innocence to be eroded by us and our sordid stories. We queers were educational. I wondered what my art school years would've been like if I'd been exposed to people like us back then.

We drove back to Oly after the show. In the van, Zee sat next to me. He nodded off to sleep, jerking awake as his head bobbed forward. Finally, I put an arm around him, pulling his head onto my shoulder to make a resting place, and he slept soundly for a while. A wash of tenderness and desire permeated the warmth of my body, where his was pressed. The sensation both confused and delighted me, a jolt of discovering something about myself that extended beyond my known comfort zone.

I had just told my friends I was trans, and I spent a good deal of the cold, endless drive from San Francisco to Olympia arguing with them about it. I was fighting the inclination to disappear from them emotionally, a default survival tactic of mine, even though I believe one of the most useful skills a person can develop is the ability to sit still in discomfort around others. My friends loved me; I knew that. I could see it in their eyes, even when they were saying, "Well, I think it's just more radical to walk the line in *between*..." or "I'll always love you, but I just don't like *men*!"

With sadness, I realized that I could be as masculine and as male-identified as humanly possible as a butch and remain accepted by my beloved dyke artist friends. But if I dared to cross that line, slip from symbolizing some kind of butch heroism into dreaded manhood, I would be excluded. I could painfully strap my chest down flat, as I'd done for more than eight years, and posture a macho swagger, but if I wanted to get the dreaded breasts cut off, or grow real sideburns, I would no longer be known to the only people who had ever felt like family to me. It felt like an awful choice.

As we neared Olympia, Zee Knuckles woke up and lifted his head off of my shoulder. In the dark of the van, as if we were totally alone, he said, "So, are you totally a straight guy or what?"

I was flustered by his forthrightness, and stammered, "Pretty much. I like the ladies, ya know?"

Zee shrugged and laid his fuzzy head back down on my shoulder. Maybe I imagined it, but it seemed like he nestled in even closer to me.

We pulled up in front of Zee's and Lola's house, and they said goodbye to us and marched up the stairs to their flat. A wild urge hit me, and I lied to my traveling companions that I needed to piss.

I dashed up the stairs two at a time and caught up with Zee at the top. I breathlessly said his name, mostly because of the smoking. I only had a minute. He turned around, and my mouth collided with his soft, red pillow lips. His tongue found its way into my mouth and my hands used his ass like a handle to pull him into my hips. It was the kind of kiss that reverberates in every cell of your body. I finally pulled away from his mouth.

"Van's leaving."

"Dude, c'mon, you're killing me," Zee said, palms out, a pained look on his face.

We kissed for a second longer, and then I turned and jogged down the stairs and got into the van for the long ride back to San Francisco, dozing off to sleep with the feel of Zee Knuckle's lips on my mouth.

Here/Now

Here, living below daylight or simply without it, the walls are red with black trim or dark blue with gold—the kind of paint job that looks fantastic at night, by candlelight, during parties, but alone there in the morning, you just want to go outside—outside, driven by a profound need for Vitamin D and clean water, the kind of water that thunders fresh through mountains, the kind they want you to believe was captured in that small plastic bottle you purchased for two dollars and are now clutching preciously in your paw. There is a certain joy in knowing hardly anyone here. There's something about parties that happen in dungeons or sex clubs that makes sex seem like the most depressing thing on earth, despite that hungry, teenaged, almost violent anticipation hanging in the air of everyone wanting sex to happen, ugly or not.

There/Then

After that one night in Olympia, short emails from Zee would appear on occasion in my Yahoo inbox. They were always bratty and flirtatious in tone, but the dramas of my own life left me with little to give to Zee's teasing pokes for attention. I fell in love with a woman in San Francisco, and when that relationship went down in flames, I was gutted. Soon, I followed the hungry, lost dog of my heartbreak right into a rebound relationship.

Feeling punched in the wound of my grief every time I left my Precita Park flat, I sublet out my room and split with the new girlfriend to Santa Fe, but not before starting hormones myself. At some point later, Zee's emails stopped. Then there were rumors. I heard things I wasn't trying to hear. Gossip is like that, flying around you, getting stuck in your head like bad music in a department store.

First, I heard Zee stopped hormones, was living as a woman again. Then it was that Zee was in Chicago, straight and dating guys, the kind who'd always been that way. Then, Zee Knuckles was strung out, a junkie or a cokehead, depending on who was gossiping. Then, Zee was turning tricks to support the habit. I never got the sense that the teller cared at all about Zee's well-being. It was just fodder, a shocking story to tell that could take the focus away from the bullshit we weren't dealing with in our own lives. I paid no attention to the gossip. Or, at least, I tried.

Here/Now

After shaking you down for some whiskey, I am ready for it, ready for anything. All of the men in skirts follow you around dotingly, like altar boys. It seems important to not want your attention, the only way to stand out in this crowd is to feign aloofness while feeling you across the room from me wherever you are; we are both positive ends of magnets, something beyond polarity. So, I just make a point of introducing myself to and conversing with the single, awkward men—clients—who pepper the party, standing out at an awkward remove from the local fauna. It surprises

me to discover that I like them. It's that karmic, one-two combo
punch when you're being a judgmental asshole and God punishes
you with love. You don't notice me noticing you checking your-
self out often in a mirror. I don't blame you; you look good, real
good—arachnid . . . in stilettos, with throwing daggers strapped
to each thigh, resting above the lip of stockings. You are an action
hero, secure inside a black patent leather exoskeleton.

At one point, a self-proclaimed marquise who looks like
George Hamilton in Love at First Bite *stands over his slave as*
she writhes on the living room floor with another woman, and
I stand behind you as you watch the women tongue each other.
You lean your superhero figure back into my chest, and I wrap my
arms around you. I think you are melting into my arms, but then
I realize that you are simply passing out on me, wasted.

There/Then

Five years after I first met Zee, I landed a job driving a truck
filled with artwork from Santa Fe galleries to a huge art expo
in Chicago. Lola was living in a basement apartment below a
palm reader, and I asked if I could crash with her for a couple days. I arrived at her place to find a warm and joyous pot-
luck dinner underway. Trans guys and dykes and queers of
all stripes were playing games and music and passing a hat to
raise some gas money for Lola's upcoming tour.

I sat on the low, broken-down sofa, wolfing down a
bowl of amorphous, anarchist, vegetarian deliciousness.

A figure dressed in black appeared at the basement door like a punk apparition, peered in the window, and turned away, disappearing down the little alleyway between Sister Rosa's Futures Told and the adjacent building. Those old rumors about Zee Knuckles bubbled to the surface of my memory—that he, now she, was living in Chicago with Lola.

"Yeah, Zee is going by Maria now, and, yeah, she lives here. She just got home from work and I forgot to tell her we were having this gathering today, so she was kinda overwhelmed when she saw all these people." Lola pointed with her chin at the gathered queerdos circled in the living room. "So she went in the back door."

I waited for what seemed like the longest hour, with a feeling of anticipation and apprehension and longing, and then asked Lola, "Can I see Zee—uh, Maria?"

Lola gestured toward a door. "Just knock," she said to me over her shoulder, and resumed her story with a friend.

I knocked.

"Yeah?"

I slowly opened the door and peered in. Maria was sitting on her bed, wearing Adidas track pants and an old punk T-shirt. Her long, black hair was wet from the shower and she was combing it.

"Oh, hey, it's you!" she said softly.

"Can I come in?" I asked. Maria nodded. I didn't close the door all the way. I didn't want to contribute to her obvious feeling of being trapped. She looked away from me, and then down at her feet. If there was somewhere to run to, she would run.

"Uh, I can leave if you want me to." I thumbed at the doorjamb beside my shoulder.

Maria's head snapped up from her close inspection of her toes. "What? Oh, no, it's okay. Sit down." She gestured to the twin bed beside her, the only place to sit in her small room besides the floor.

Even though it was tiny and modest, the room still felt sensuous and full of mystery. There were dark red scarves thrown over the lamps, giving off an opium den glow. A votive candle flickered on a dresser with a 1920s vanity mirror on it, the Virgin Mary dancing in the flame's glow. Music was playing softly, something dark and sexy, maybe Radiohead. Pictures covered the walls, strange collages of women Maria made from cosmetic ads, oversized lips superimposed over black-and-white nude models.

I noticed a set of wrist cuffs peeking out between the head-board of her bed and the mattress. I *love* femme bedrooms.

Here/Now

But most of the night, you ignore me because you think I'll be there waiting for you at the end, when everyone else has gone home. I laugh at myself when I am, but by then you are passed out and I am lying beside you, fully clothed. Boots and all—awake, listening to your thick, slow breathing cascading into snoring and smoothing back out again, struck with an epiphany that I have been here before—not with you, but at least one other. Back then, I felt grateful to lie beside the passed-out form of a woman I found beautiful, like some large and loyal dog kept close for warmth and protection, but that was a long time ago and now I am just careful not to want anything. I peel your drunk ass out of your black leather shell so you can breathe, your body visibly expanding with oxygen before you pass out.

There/Then

Maria told me that it was hard for her to see people from "back then." She was afraid I wouldn't accept her. I could smell her hair and her light, musky perfume. I was aware of my own shifting shape, the awkward, in-between state of myself, and the weight of it all bearing down on her bed. "I'm the last person who's going to judge you for your gender expression, you know?" I said. She looked at me through impossibly thick eyelashes.

We talked for a while about the past few years and about some mutual friends. I mentioned the gossip.

"I didn't give much credence to it." It sounded like a lie as soon as I said it.

"Well, some of it is grounded in truth, I guess," she said. She looked down again, safe beneath the shadow of those eyelashes. "My first couple of years here were bad. I was in a relationship with this guy, it was bad news. I was using a lot. Now I'm domming in this dungeon, but the owners make us sub too, sometimes. I don't like it, but the money is too good to pass up." She peered through the hair that had fallen down over her face. She was being so vulnerable with me, and yet, to acknowledge this seemed like it would scare her off. I hoped my face broadcasted the empathy I felt while listening to her. "I got clean and stopped hanging out with my ex and his friends. I moved in with Lola. Things are better now."

Later that night, we all gathered in the living room and played Mafia. She was hilarious, sarcastic, and witty, much more vocal than I remembered Zee ever being. I sat on the couch, and at some point, she leaned back against my legs from where she was sitting on the floor, claiming me. I could feel electricity run up my legs with each breath she took. She cracked jokes to the group through those still-unbelievable lips and hooked an arm over my knees. Her scent wafted up to my nostrils, and I had to resist leaning down to put my nose in her black hair to breathe in her delicious smell. I was hyperconscious of the curve of her ass through her black dress against my boot.

Eventually, Lola was tired and kicked everyone else out. Maria and I sat in the living room talking until 2 a.m.

"I'm going to bed," she yawned. "You can stay there on the couch or come sleep with me." She got up without waiting for an answer. I followed her, propelled by a current of nebulous desire, and curled up in her tiny bed with her. I wasn't sure what we were doing, what *I* was doing.

But then she pushed her ass into my crotch when I spooned her. Do we contain want in our bodies, within the corporeal meat we lug around through our days, or is desire something more animal or electric? Somewhere between the passing trajectories of our genders, the ghost of that Olympia kiss glowed alive and shapeless between us. I pressed my hips closer and wound a heavy arm around her.

I thought about the awful relationship I'd left moldering back in Santa Fe, with a girlfriend who cheated on me with our mutual friends and macraméd convoluted lies, defending her actions by telling everyone I was a horrible person. Meanwhile, I'd done a great job of interpellating the messaging of our culture: Embarking upon this transition meant that I was shoving off from the shore of lovability, that I was in fact worthless, and so I stayed with her. And in the few instances where things got so bad that I tried to leave, my girlfriend would beg me to stay, plead to not be left by me, telling me how much she loved me and needed me. I blamed myself for becoming so vulnerable and too weak to jump off the carnival ride of my lackluster choices. For some reason, I felt compelled to maintain my thin ledge of moral high ground where my relationship was concerned, despite my longing for connection now in this too-small bed.

"Maria?"

"Mmm-hmmm," she mumbled.

"Look, I want you, but right now, I just can't."

Maria rolled over and kissed my eyebrow, nonplussed. She hadn't made any demands of me, after all. She turned back over and was soon snoring. I lay in the dark, my right arm falling asleep under her, pounding with longing so hard I felt my pulse in my eardrums.

Maria went to work at the dungeon the next morning. She woke me up with a phone call, asking me to look up some references to Victorian sadomasochism in a book of hers, inspiration for a schoolteacher scene with a client. I read her some choice passages from the well-worn volume, and we laughed a lot. Maybe I'd been overthinking everything through the unreliable narrator of my broken, bewildered heart. I packed my bag, ready for my long haul back to New Mexico.

Here/Now

You are inconsistent and probably full of shit, but this only exacerbates your big, messy heart, rather than obscuring it. Try to unravel the physics behind this phenomenon: It's like how lightning actually travels from the ground to the sky, but visually, it looks to be the reverse. You don't deserve my patience, but I give it to you regardless. You flit and flicker from branch to branch, a hungry sparrow gathering crumbs of attention from everyone at the party. You seem so radically different from the last time I saw you that I assume you are using, that you are high.

I am reveling in the freedom of not belonging here, of not belonging to anyone. My best relationship has been with possibility, with potential—mine or anyone else's. There are no ex-lovers, no one I would rather not see. Just some acquaintances and some new friends and a whole lot of possibility.

Did you know that I am hard to know? That I am a loner? That I can be all work and no play? That I don't know how to fuck without intimacy anymore, and truthfully, I don't know if I would want to? Been-there-done-that makes things like tenderness and intimacy feel like radical acts. Did you know that when she left, she took with her the expansiveness of my heart? I mean, it broke me. I mean, I am broken. The me that followed you, back when you were a boy, up the stairwell to your apartment in Olympia and slammed you with a huge, faggot, might-as-well-have-fucked-it-was-so-hot kiss—yeah, that guy—sometimes I think he's a ghost. He's so pale and far away, not quite of this world anymore. I was still getting carded for cigarettes, even though I was in my early thirties, and overnight I looked my age, my youthfulness as a mirror or metaphor of the openness of my heart, broken and bringing me seven years' shitty luck. And now, here I am in your bedroom—again, safe because I've convinced myself I'm not invested in the outcome. For I'm just as lost, I'm just as fucked and forsaken as you are.

There/Then

I received a ten-page letter from Maria a few weeks later. She wrote that she couldn't remember if we very first met in a smoky bar or underwater, but that she could never forget that kiss. That I was a reminder of her life back when she felt like she could give a shit about herself or anyone else or her art. That seeing me was a reminder that not everyone was out to fuck over everyone else. That those feelings for me reminded her that even Zee once had that kind of innocence within. And that she wished we'd made love that night.

Here/Now

I am not sure which one of us is better at pretending we are okay. You get angry and indignant when I ask, saying, "I am Fine. I am Fine." With a palm, you whisk the trail of crumbs that you left for me to find you off your sheetless bed. You ask me if I know what it means to be in your bed. I don't know what it means for you, so tell me—if you even know yourself. To have me in your bed means I believed in you, at least a little bit, even if you didn't expect me to.

My story: We first met in the damp underground, surrounded by strings of lights and blown-out amps, not in a smoky bar or underwater. So, tell me. Tell me your story of how you met me—I'd rather it be interesting than truthful, if there has to be a choice. Slaves are getting ass-fucked out in your living room on the hardwood floor, a show for the straights. The pros and scruffy trans and queers are now stuffed precariously onto a balcony, violating building code, smoking cigarettes and getting into more interesting mischief.

Here in your bedroom, we don't know what it means to lie beside each other. How to negotiate the people we were then with the people we are now. The not-knowing is the lowest common denominator. In the dark, your room is red, warm, and sinewy, like the inside of an organ, but by morning, as sunshine and city street noise assaults the windows, I will want to drag you out of here. Push you into daylight. Unlike all of the other vampires here, I want to give you your blood back.

There/Then

I hid the letter from my girlfriend. Some inchoate part of me believed a lying, friend-fucking woman was what I deserved. In this loneliness, Maria Zee's letter was a lifeline—a mirror, someone who understood my journey and who felt just as alone and confused. I read that letter over and over.

Some months later, Lola invited me back to Chicago to perform at her monthly queer performance night at a local sex toy shop. Spoken word with a backdrop of fleshy dildoes and pink and purple butt plugs. I wrote to Maria, said that I really wanted to see her while I was in town. She wrote back to tell me she was now living with another friend in her apartment/dungeon, a true live/work situation. She wanted to see me, too. She offered to throw a party at the dungeon to help pay my way to Chicago.

When/Where

Within two weeks, it will be difficult to ascertain that this ever happened—whatever it is. I will remember, for the first time in my life, sharing a bed with another person who knows empirically how it feels to have body parts that don't belong and ones that may never be there, that every sexual act knocks you against incongruity, out of which you may never carve resolve.

You unfold my arms crossed over my bare chest, and say, "Do you think you need to explain that to me?" But you can't take a piece out of the puzzle and still have a picture. Within two weeks, I'll be working on a construction site, placing joists to roof a house and remembering you straddling me with your thighs tight around me, my back against the red bedroom wall, kissing the thick scars across your chest that trace the map of your journey to male and back again. Waves of want in between the incessant, pounding beats of the pneumatic nailer. I will be back in the high desert, thirsty—not belonging here, either, but not knowing where else to go.

The First Time

For Kris Kovick

Even though I'm grown, I've always wanted an adult I could count on. I've never been a joiner. I've never thrown in my lot with anyone else's. The news came early on in life that I was on my own. But still, the desire to have someone to turn to, of whom I could ask for advice, persists.

You love my paintings. You believe in me as an artist more than I ever have. You respect that I work hard—like you—in a shop all day, squeezing in your life as an artist and writer somewhere between work and sleep.

You once said to me, the context of the conversation long-gone, "That's because you're a transsexual." And I felt seen. Seen because we held up mirrors to each other. A hallway from mirror to mirror looking inward forever. I felt believed. Believed, and relieved, and recognized. You laughed kindly when you said it, and I was amazed that you could be so casual about seeing who I was. Not creepy, like this straight woman at work, who, when the UPS guy called me "bro" and I obviously enjoyed it, asked me if I had

"Brandon Teena syndrome." With you, my gender identity isn't a big deal—it simply is, like the Earth simply is, like the sky is simply sky.

YOU ALREADY had cancer when we became close. You distracted yourself from your betraying, painful body, talking to me under your lemon tree about my broken heart. I mean, I was shattered. *How do you reconfigure your self-identity when it was based on the enormity of your heart, and suddenly you find yourself with a raisin-sized organ rattling around in your dusty ribcage?* You, on a lawn chair with plump lemons sinking the branches down low, were butch royalty, a King. With tears in your eyes, you told me, "This is what getting through things looks like."

I watched you fight back tears, your lower eyelids Hoover Dams, choking back a river of hard luck and anguish. Trying to make it easy on all of us by not bitching, ever, even when you were in dire pain. You try to give me your morphine pills when I tweak my back at work, pills you really need. That day, holding court under the lemon tree, I knew you weren't going to be here much longer. Bittersweet impermanence, the ephemeral, fleeting beauty in life—you are a cherry blossom, like the ones tattooed on my left forearm, reminding me that nothing lasts, everything changes. Nothing lasts. There is nothing to hold onto.

I picture you in the park, shovel in hand, scooping other people's dogs' shit deftly into a brown paper grocery sack, the edge neatly rolled down. "Working off my karmic deficit," you called it.

You gave me a key to your house and said, "If you're ever sad, or lonely…" You fed me sandwiches, sliced-in-half croissants shiny with butter, toasted with cheese, and filled with sautéed mushrooms and smoked turkey breast. Barbecued chicken wings marinated for days in lime juice and soy sauce. Baked potatoes like ice cream sundaes, topped with butter and sour cream and sprinkles of chopped, crispy bacon, green onions, and coarse black pepper. Thin, verdant stalks of asparagus al dente, with Parmesan cheese tossed over lightly as snowflakes. Steaks. Vast slabs of grilled meat, juicy and languorous, draped over the greater part of the plate like a grand odalisque. Cakes, usually chocolate, because why fuck around with anything else?

After devouring one of these meals, you said of Sini and me, "Man, you boys can eat!" But it wasn't only our bellies you were feeding. You nourished us with something we'd been hungry for our whole lives: family. Once, I said you were like a father to me. You said you worked hard to be a good father to yourself. This could be the greatest thing you ever taught me.

YOU NEVER accepted my attempts to return your generosity. If I hadn't been so broken, so lost, it would've pissed me off. I would've refused further kind deeds from you until you allowed me to help you out in some way. Instead, I lay in the bed of chamomile you'd planted in your garden, or in bed with you and your girlfriend, who never complained when I fell asleep fifteen minutes into a movie, snoring beside the two of you.

She told me that "workshopping my broken heart" really made you feel useful, needed. I believe this, truly, but there's another layer. If you are extremely paternal, generous, and giving, yet don't allow anyone to do kind things for you, you limit your chances for disappointment. You keep control.

IT'S FUNNY how you talked about suicide for more than a year and everyone around you knew, but when you finally did it, everything fell apart. These disparate souls you gathered are mismatched and random without the mortar of your presence. Despite your plans to take your own life, it's amazing how much people still resisted your death, how they argued with each other and themselves about how you weren't really as bad off as you seemed, how you didn't need to go. They argued about how your death was wrong, how you shouldn't have, how the cancer was still treatable. They argued about the whereabouts of your lucky coin necklace, your most recently purchased shoes, your manuscript, even who should stay in your house.

I am alone in your bedroom, crying, sitting cross-legged on the rug, eyeing your black horn-rimmed glasses on your pillow, empty of you. Exactly where you were lying the last time I saw you, just a couple days before, in your silk pajamas and old-man glasses—handsome, looking more like a 1950s movie star than a dying person.

You exercised the ultimate control, no surprise except for the surprise that it still fucking hurts, no matter how much I thought I'd prepared. I fear that you secretly resented me for accepting your generosity of spirit. Had I failed an unspoken test of character by taking you up on your kindness? Did I not exercise enough control?

I push my hands into the hot, soapy water and wash your dishes slowly, thoroughly, lingering on the weight of each dish in my hands. I scrub the tines of each fork carefully because I know that the sight of dirty silverware made you nauseous. Really, this is why you never let anyone wash your dishes, even me, no matter how much I joke about my professional experience as a hydro-ceramic technician or how often I expounded upon my philosophy of the kitchen and its pursuant golden rule: If someone cooks for you, you wash the dishes. No amount of cajoling or charm could sway you. But now, I wash your dishes painstakingly, meditatively. I am only getting away with it because you died today.

Sharing Trans:
Internet Transgender Discourses
and the End of Gatekeeping

Author's note: I researched and wrote this piece in 2013, and I include it in this book, not only for the shards of trans history it contains, but also because it points to the swiftness in which the trans community has evolved in the six years since I wrote it.

"We can easily imagine a culture where discourse would circulate without any need for an author."
—MICHEL FOUCAULT

I. What We Talk about
When We Talk to Each Other

I received a Facebook email message yesterday. At first, I didn't know who it was from, but after a little profile-scouring, I determined the sender was a young adult from New Mexico, a friend of students with whom I'd closely worked as a program coordinator for a state-wide LGBTQ and ally youth leadership development program. We'd probably met once or twice at some event.

Hello everyone! This is a mass announcement (sent to 225 people) *to all of my FB friends about something very important happening right now in my life. I recently began the physical transition from "female" to "male," by starting on testosterone injections.*

I'd love to talk to each and every one of you about this if you're interested. If so, please send me a separate PRIVATE message. (Please, please don't respond to this message because it will alert everyone on the list, and I don't want to annoy anyone with too many messages!)

In addition, I've begun making videos chronicling this transition, as well as just putting some of my ideas about life out there in the world. I'm going to be starting an email list to alert people when I make a video. If you would be interested in receiving one, send me a SEPARATE message with your email address. I'll remove you from the list whenever you want, and will never share your email with anyone else, ever.

If it is easier for you, you can also just subscribe to me on YouTube by copying and pasting the following link. Thank you so much for taking the time to read this, and know that I really appreciate all the support I have received from everyone in this process so far.

Once upon a time, most of my Facebook friends were friends and family, the queer underground, writing and arts community contacts, and other acquaintances—people whom I'd actually met, had a relationship to, worked on projects with, or whose couch I'd crashed on while on book tour. After I hit about 2000 "friends," this was no longer the case. These days, I have countless connections to younger trans people who might have read something I wrote once and asked to be friends. I say yes, usually out of a sense of community responsibility, of being there for those who come after me. I owe a lot to those who've packed down the deep snow on this trail before me.

This Facebook message exemplified a particular trans discourse generated from within the trans community from people of a certain age and cultural demographics. Transitions are now happenings—something others can subscribe to, participate in, and even help to fund—via the Internet. Things have changed a lot since I began my own process of transition in 2002.

I ENCOUNTERED female-to-male transgender and transsexual people for the first time when I moved to San Francisco in 1993. I'd crossed paths with people who transgressed gender norms going the other direction during my summers working multiple jobs in Provincetown, Massachusetts to gather tuition money for my undergraduate program at Massachusetts College of Art. There was a significant overlap between the community of drag performers and transfeminine people who performed drag in P-town that seemed pretty damn fluid compared to the stark distinctions folks have tried to pry between those worlds in recent years. Previously, I'd been oblivious to the possibility of transition for myself, although I had always felt misaligned; the articulations and presentations of gender that felt the most authentic and comfortable to me were regularly responded to with criticism, outrage, insult, consternation, confusion, and at times abuse or outright violence, not to mention the non-articulated feedback that I perceived just as strongly, which was perhaps more maddening for its lack of specificity.

I knew innately that the body I was in seemed a mismatch, an alien exterior that I felt bad complaining about since it was healthy and functional in every way. It just never matched the image of myself in my mind, to the extent that sometimes I would find myself surprised by it, as if an imposter had come and swapped bodies with me while I was showering, only for me to discover the trick while I was toweling dry. It was the hand I'd been dealt, I'd tell myself (admitting these thoughts to no one) and there was nothing I could do about it. Or so I thought. As Susan Stryker so eloquently states: "Gender is a percussive symphony of automatisms, reverberating through the space of our bodies before there is an awareness of awareness itself. Who can say why I heard its music the way I did?"[1]

I WAS overwhelmed by seeing and meeting FTMs for the first time in San Francisco. The idea of going through a tortuous process to access medical intervention to change my body, and *then change my body* felt monumental, stressful, insurmountable. Like many kids who grew up in dysfunctional households, I perceived the unhappy known to be much less scary than the possibly-healthy unknown, having honed a staunch ability to endure. Coming to an identity of *queer* wasn't that hard for me; it was a piece of information that clicked into place and clarified things. It made so much of why I felt so different—so off—make sense. But if a transsexual was what I was, then it wasn't a matter of just who I desired. It was *who* I was, the outer shell of me, the functioning of my brain and chemical drivetrain of my endocrine system, would undergo enormous change, as would my face, body, voice, temperament, and social location from deep within a Neverland of queers and dyke artists. It would all change. How the world interfaced with me, and I with it, would change. Change was terrifying, especially when the outcome was a crapshoot.

I remembered reading an ominous anecdote written somewhere by a trans man in an FTM newsletter: "You can choose to become a man, but you can't choose the man you will become." In 1993, most of the handful of trans men that I was aware of transitioned to male and then vacated the nest of the queer community to live stealth lives in that world out there. The idea terrified me. *Would I be expected to go through all of this just to hide the history of who I am again?*

In 1993, people who wanted to transition were often still forced into undertaking what was known as "the Real-Life

Test," which would run from three months to two years, based on the discretion of whichever authority the person got stuck dealing with. In this time period, designated by one's psychiatrist or therapist, you were expected to live as your "chosen" gender—that is, you were expected to adopt your new name, new pronouns, and live "full-time" as your new self without the aid of medical intervention, and interface with your life as a trans person. The RLT forced people, all at once, to parachute from identity into their social, familial, and working worlds as a "new" self, with nothing to prepare for the landing or pad the impact. We might call this "transitioning socially" now, except it isn't so common that people will go about transition quite in the same way as the Real-Life Test pushed for.

The RLT enforced a strict gender binary as well. It worked against trans people who were bi, gay, lesbian, and queer. The test was like a Play-Doh Fun Factory that tried to push people through a die, forcing them to inhabit recognizable and normative shapes on the other end. It was a method of gatekeeping, a psychological endurance test: If you could survive it without going crazy, giving up, or getting killed, you would prove that this gender business was serious, that it was *real*, and you would get a letter from your mental health provider finally approving you for hormones or surgery. Getting access to them was another story. The Real-Life Test seems archaic, even cruel, now.

I had a roommate back then who went from being a

swaggering, pompadoured, butch dyke to a different person overnight (as it seemed to those of us outside of his brain). Like a switch had flipped one day, we all had to start calling him "him," and a new name: Marco. Suddenly, Marco was somehow even gruffer than before, and his speech became instantly monosyllabic. He seemed to never smile again and talked with his chin tucked into his neck. He packed every day with an almost pornographic prosthesis and pasted on big sideburns. His physical movements, even his walk, became exaggerated, punchier. He tossed out all of his fabulous three-piece suits and wore only oversized work shirts and Ben Davis pants. Overnight, he went from looking like a male movie star in a Martin Scorsese film to a gas station attendant.

He was required to show up at work like this one day and announce that he was now Marco and present this way henceforth. He had to prove to all of his world that he could carry this "male role" on his own two shoulders, without any help from doctors or shrinks—he had to work hard to convince everyone that he was "male enough" and gender dysphoric enough to merit "the change." This structure, placed on Marco from outside by a system holding the power to his embodied happiness, seemed arbitrary, unfair, silly, and also like a gross reinforcement of gender stereotypes, not to mention a binary. Heterosexuality was assumed to be mandatory. For Marco to be seen as truly male, or worthy of becoming male, in the confines of the RLT, he had to pantomime exaggerated codes of what "male" meant, what "male" looked like. The psychological discourses of power had, of course, an imperative to keep and enforce a gender binary. If you are not this (female) you must be this (male), and these are the prescribed manners in which these two options may be expressed.

Passing the Real-Life Test did not mean success. It meant that you had satisfied the regimes of power, who held the keys to your transition in their parsimonious hands, by jumping through their arbitrary hoops of gender normativity.

I found the Real-Life Test terrifying. I'm grateful that I was never forced to participate in it.

Even in the early 1990s, getting your information wasn't easy. The examples that follow largely bear on the FTM end of things, as that's where my personal journey took me. I can't offer much about how all of this was working (or not) for trans women since that was not my experience, and for reasons that are beyond the scope of this essay to explore, these two paths are often and unfortunately very segregated. By the late 1990s, transgender resources were cropping up all over the web, making a huge shift in ease of access to information. If finding information and resources wasn't easy in San Francisco, it must have been downright near impossible in less urban and progressive places. Before those early sites and chat rooms, access to subjugated knowledge was limited to a few hard-to-find books, pamphlets, and possibly support group meetings if one were lucky enough to live in a large metro area. Early informational websites were simply-coded pages of lists and links, mostly directing questioning and trans people to resources along the medical/psycho/juridical complex, but some cropped up that explored the trans narrative subjectively and even artistically.

Gwendolyn Ann Smith, creator of Transgender Day of Remembrance and the site "Remembering Our Dead," both of which honor transgender people who have been killed due to trans discrimination and hatred, states that, "It wasn't until the early 1990s that transgender activism as we know it today really began to take hold, and the transgender community has the Internet to thank." She credits the Internet for giving trans people worldwide access to information, where previously, "communication was based on sporadic periodicals and word of mouth."[2]

Smith received her first America Online (AOL) disk in the mail in early 1993 and found her first transgender chat room, called TV Chat. A long-time computer expert and web-mistress, Smith was active early on in having "transsexual" and "transvestite" removed from AOL's list of "vulgar" words. She began to provide trans-related resources and information on the web in 1995. She helped to create and host the online presence of trans photographer and icon Loren Cameron, who is well-known for his book *Body Alchemy*,[3] which was an enormously influential book for many trans men of my generation; for many of us, it was the first time we saw possibilities for who we could be reflected back to us in art. Both Gwen Smith and scholar Eve Shapiro allude to the anonymity of the Internet allowing trans people to access information, self-education, political organizing, and resources without having to take public risks of exposure. Shapiro encourages us to see the role of the Internet in present-day trans organizing as two-fold: The Internet is both a "tool" and a "space."[4]

There were a few well-known books that you might find at the gay and lesbian bookstore in the Castro in the pre-search engine days: There was the glum-looking yet informative *Masculinizing Hormone Therapy for the Transgendered* by Sheila Kirk, M.D., for instance, or you might glimpse a peek at FTM characters in *Stone Butch Blues* or the erotic fiction of Pat(rick) Califia. You might find a flyer for a support group tacked up in that bookstore or maybe a coffee shop or hear about it through word-of-mouth. FTM International published a print quarterly newsletter that got snail-mailed around the globe. FTM meetings took place in San Francisco; a flyer only had the dates of the monthly meeting and a landline number that you had to call. You'd have to leave a message on the answering machine to receive the address after you were somewhat vetted as appropriate to attend. The T was still a tenuous, even contentious, addition to the LGB, and it was unsafe to post the time and location of a gathering of female-to-male transgender people back then, even in San Francisco.

I WASN'T ready to embark upon my own transition for a very long time. I did things slowly, piecemeal. I changed my first name in 1997, both socially and common-law legally (pre-9/11, it was fairly easy to change your name on your driver's license in California), then in 1999 I started asking lovers and close friends to use male pronouns for me. My masculine presentation didn't change much, it just *meant* differently. I bound my chest most of the time.

In 2001, I went to a public health clinic in the Tenderloin to get a prescription for hormones. I went to where I wouldn't have to be questioned too hard or have to educate: the Tom Waddell Clinic on "Tranny Tuesday." I filled out my intake form and waited in a dreary, poorly lit hallway with mostly transfeminine people in cheap orange plastic chairs. The Real-Life Test was not a requirement at Tom Waddell, but I gave my narrative to the intake clinician—a version of my life that I knew instinctively I had to render down to the most obvious clues to my "true" masculine self, essentializing all my variegations and experiences down to distilled points of "male." I had to profess hatred for body parts that I felt neutral about or simply detached from. I had to embrace a sense of gender black-and-whites in a manner that ran against the grain of my queer sensibilities. I had to accentuate that my first doll was a G.I. Joe and neglect to mention that my second doll was a Barbie. This version of my story was by no means untrue, but it was a story of my life told in fewer dimensions than in which it was actually lived:

It was the version of my story that I needed to tell in order to receive the medical interventions that I wanted.

II. (Virtual) Hirstories of Embodiment

To learn more, I reached out to two figures instrumental to my own trans awakening, Dr. Susan Stryker and Dr. Jordy Jones, both of whom were situated in the nexus of San Francisco queer culture, art, performance, activism, kink, and trans identity. They're of a trans generation that just preceded mine. I wanted to learn how they found trans community and what they are noticing now about how we talk to and find needed resources—and each other. One of my favorite things about each scholar's respective responses to my questions is how they illustrate the fact that language *means* so differently to each of us hanging out beneath that so-called umbrella.

IN "(De)Subjugated Knowledges," the introduction to *The Transgender Studies Reader*, Susan Stryker mentions the rapid proliferation of the term "transgender" in the mid-1990s, fueled by the explosion of the World Wide Web.[5] This struck a chord with me—I've often wondered if the Internet is one of the greatest things that's ever happened to trans people. Susan references a graph from *The Transgender Studies Reader Vol. 2* that depicts the occurrences of the word "transgender" in books scanned into Google. She says, "Since about 1992, *transgender* has experienced a meteoric rise in popularity compared to other familiar terms for describing gender nonconforming practices.[6] The image clearly marks the trajectory of the term—in fact, from 1990 to 2010, the line is nearly vertical."

Jordy Jones: "Transgender" as a term is still contested as hell. Its use as a political/legislative term and as an identity category overlap, but also diverge. It is entirely possible to qualify as transgender under policy verbiage (i.e., insurance) but not identify as transgender per se. The explosion of the term in the 1990s meant that there was a handy name under which many different kinds of people could be categorized. This was needed for policy work but truncates the complexity of individuals and our lives.

Cooper Lee Bombardier: I'm interested in exploring how the rise of the Internet has shifted the center of power in transgender discourses from medical/legal-dominant discourses to a decentralized, peer-based system of information exchange. I'd like to consider both the pros and cons of this shift. I'm interested in how widespread access to anecdotal and experiential information-sharing has changed the nature of the transgender narrative and the language used, and if/how this decentralizing shift has reified into and changed the language of the power discourses.

Susan Stryker: I think this is absolutely right, that the Internet was crucial for the ongoing shift of trans discourse away from the medical model. I remember, back in the late '80s/early '90s, how clear it was what the target needed to be, in terms of bringing a more radical/queer sensibility to bear on gender transformation. I remember feeling so pissed off that it was so difficult to access trans communities, and the ways the med/psych service providers controlled access much more than they do now. I remember thinking, *If somebody was questioning whether or not they were gay, they would just go to the Castro or the Mission, or the White Horse* [an East Bay lesbian bar], *or whatever, and hook up and find out if that was their cup of tea—find out from other people who lived their lives that way*. And it pissed me off that the therapists wouldn't steer people towards trans communities or community-based knowledge. I remember how hard I had to work to find something trans that wasn't a support group taking place in some social service-y setting. I could find really exploitative tranny sex-worker spaces, I could find pretty sad/underattended support groups, I could find therapists, and that was about it until this new queer scene started up in the context of AIDS activism, anti-war activism, kink, etc. I remember feeling around 1993, when attending the National March for LGB Rights, that I knew every single person in the U.S. who was doing trans activism of any kind. And then Netscape came along.[7]

CLB: Do either of you see a relationship between the rapid proliferation of the term "transgender" and the widespread use of the World Wide Web, or is this a coincidence?

SS: I do think it was kind of a coincidence. I mean, there was a new sociocultural formation emerging that "transgender" came to name just before the proliferation of the Internet, that I think happened for all the reasons I outlined in "(De)Subjugated Knowledges," and that term happened to be the one in vogue when the Internet hit, that all the tech-savvy kids were using.

CLB: What role do each of you think the rise of the Web plays in terms of the huge leaps in visibility the trans community has made in the past two decades?

JJ: The Web plays a huge role in visibility. "Huge leaps" makes it sound like visibility is a good thing. In many ways, it is. It's certainly usually presented as a positive. Certainly, connectivity has positive functional uses, including resource-sharing and "peer-based" systems of knowledge exchange. On the downside, dubious opinions that go viral can quickly become subcultural "facts." Private individuals find themselves as "subject lines" in public chat rooms, discussed by peers and strangers. Connectivity does not require visibility, but with the advent of social media, they are usually coupled. Visibility has become semi-compulsory, and efforts made by individuals to maintain personal privacy are sometimes cast as "bad for" some imaginary ideal of community. I'd like to see the notion of privacy given a fraction of the consideration that the notion of visibility is.

SS: Well, I think you say it yourself—the Web played a huge role in terms of visibility. There was a *New York Times* article from about 1995 that makes this point, about the relationship between transgender/Web/visibility. I think the same sort of dynamic pertained to lots of other, previously more isolated/marginalized/dispersed communities and identities. Just in general, the Web connected people in ways that were previously impossible, decentered networks on scales previously impossible.

CLB: What has been the effect of the Internet on transgender discourses?

SS: Heteroglossia. Fractal complexity. Audience segmentation.

CLB: In your opinion, has the availability of trans-related information and access to resources via the Internet shifted the power in transgender discourse away from a medical/psycho/juridical center to a decentralized, peer-based system of exchange? If so, what do you see as the pros and cons of this shift?

SS: Well, I'm loathe to say that it's a con, though admittedly it makes organizing difficult, and results in people talking past each other in really stupid ways sometimes. It's just how trans discourse is organized now. The argument you are making about the proliferation of trans discourses propelling the shift away from medical/psycho/juridical is exactly the same that I make about "trans studies" versus "studies of transgenderism." I'm really trying to help create a context in which the med/psych model is just one discourse among many, rather than it being in a position of dominance. The deeply political rationale behind *TSQ: Transgender Studies Quarterly* is to have a different kind of "expert discourse" that further contests pathologizing and othering discourses on trans.

CLB: Has the advent of trans-initiated information in turn informed discourses of medical/psycho/juridical professionals who used to regulate the form and content of these dialogues?

SS: Less than I would have hoped for, other than HBIGDA/WPATH[8] co-opting the term "transgender" in the title their journal, *IJT*.

CLB: I think of the rapid adoption of the term "cisgender" from within the trans community, and now we see that term used widely. In other words, have our discourses changed the way we are, in turn, talked about?

SS: I think this is certainly becoming true in public discourse, in the mass media and in social media. But there is still a medicalized discourse that carries great authority, particularly in countries where there is some sort of nationalized healthcare system and trans medical services are state-funded.

JJ: I think you may be overestimating the effect of trans-specific language on the greater culture, including related subcultures. I would be very surprised if many of my friends, most of whom are cisgender men, have ever heard of the word. Trans people and "allies" all know it.

CLB: Has the exponential increase of trans presence on the Internet—from the early, most basic resource websites and listservs to the blogosphere and beyond—changed the nature of transgender narrative and transgender language, either what is employed from within the community about ourselves or from outside of our community about us?

SS: Yes, of course. Sounds like maybe you are headed toward your own research topic here, for a thesis or dissertation? This is a very big question.

CLB: In "(De)Subjugated Knowledges," Susan discusses in great detail the extent to which trans people were objects to be written about by institutions of power. Now that transgender studies is a viable multidisciplinary field, trans people have been able to enter these discourses and wed lived experience to theory in unprecedented ways. Have we shifted the conversation away from being objects of study? Will we always be subjected to regimes of power which attempt to normalize and control? Or do we continue to "[taunt] the social order" as you say? Do *we* turn ourselves and other trans people into objects?

SS: The question you raise is really important. I think everybody within modernity is the target of various regimes of power that have normativizing subjectification as their aim. My own hope is that trans studies is part of a critical practice that alerts us to ways in which, through analysis and critique, we can find ways to exercise agency and resist domination within these regimes of power, by influencing and redirecting the pathways through which power flows.

JJ: In pursuing a career as a professional trans person, we certainly can turn ourselves into our own academic subject. This is true of many of the galaxy of "studies." In academia, we can become "collectible"—hired to represent our presumed identity category, in addition to teaching within our discipline.

CLB: What are significant points on the timeline of transgender presence on the Web as you recall? In other words, what sites stand out to you as crucial or influential (I think of Gwen Smith's "Remembering Our Dead," or the FTM_Trans Yahoo listserv/group I am still part of, which has been in existence since 1999).[9]

SS: One that was really significant for me was the trans-academic listserv that came out of the 1993 or '94 Queer Studies Conference in Iowa City. There were a bunch of us there who came to that conference specifically because we thought we would meet people who were doing queer-inflected trans academic work, taking it as a matter of faith that we were not the only ones in the world. Turns out there were 20+ people who came to the transgender caucus meeting, and we sent a list around the room to collect emails, and the listserv was born.

JJ: Some Kind of Queer—2001. The Trannyfags listserv started around 1995. [Web] art: *Brandon*, Virtual Guggenheim, by Shu Lea Cheang, et al. 1997 [restored by Guggenheim in 2017]. Stafford has run the FTM surgery info lists for about a decade. Some big general LGBT blogs are "transier" than others—Bilerico Project vs. Towleroad, for instance.

CLB: I recently read an article in *The New Yorker*, "About a Boy: Transgender Surgery at Sixteen."[10] Author Margaret Talbot seems to be an ally, but there are still insidious ways in which heteronormativity, gender essentialism, and gender normativity inform the entire article. I was particularly struck by the ways in which she used "our" language—that is, language that trans people coin and use about ourselves—in quotes, but used language that we might consider problematic (enter the dreaded sex change) without the qualifying and distancing quotes. Talbot goes on to cite young people's confessional transition video diaries on YouTube, and even books and television with trans characters as a causality for the "phenomena" of more and more people identifying as trans, at earlier and earlier ages.

SS: Couple of things—there's an article by Mel Chen called

"Everywhere Archives" in an issue of *Australian Feminist Studies* around 2009 that looks at Asian FTMs' use of YouTube videos to build up a "transition archive." And there's [Tobias Raun] who just finished his dissertation at Roskilde University in Denmark on YouTube as a "how-to" resource for transitioning.

CLB: I'll check those out, thank you. In effect, Talbot seems to portray transgender people's ability to communicate directly with each other—cutting out the arbitrating medical/scientific regimes that in the past served as regulators and gatekeepers—as spreading the identity of *transgender* as some sort of "contagion." That by having a voice, all we need is an audience, and another unsuspecting tomboy girl or sissy boy will be recruited as one of us. Can you speak to this idea of causality and fear around transgender discourses "creating" new trans people?

SS: Well, you do a pretty good job here yourself. I thought that article definitely had an undercurrent of anxiety.

CLB: Do you think there is any validity in Talbot's (article's) anxiety about people transitioning at younger and younger ages?

SS: You know, I do wonder sometimes if some folks now might later regret trans medical interventions the way they might regret tattoos. But most folks don't seem to have any regrets about tattoos or transitions. I admit I feel a little ambivalent about young transitioners sometimes. On the one hand, I know quite clearly that

I would have done it if I could have. And I see the ones I've had a chance to see as being really happy. I know that if somebody said to me when I was three or four or five that it was OK for me to be a girl and I could be one if that's what I wanted, there would have been no hesitation in me. And yet at the same time, I really value the queer political perspective I've gained from living a more gender-discordant life. My worry is not so much that the people who do transition really young will regret it, so much as it is that something beautiful about the trans/genderqueer experience will be lost.

But at the same time, I acknowledge that this is simply the ambivalence that comes with age and the recognition that the circumstances that have shaped your own life are themselves fleeting, and that the conditions that formed you inevitably change, rendering your achievements and challenges largely incomprehensible and irrelevant to many of those who come after you. Such is life, and that's okay.

Maybe a bigger worry is that early transitioning has a lot to do with the anxieties of the parents, and an uncomfortableness with gender discordance.

CLB: The very subtitle of the article seeks to capitalize on this anxiety. Is there any risk to transgender discourses becoming too exposed, normalized, mainstream? Any risk that we will become "defanged," no longer "taunting to the social order"?

SS: One of the points I tried to make in my 1994 article on Frankenstein[11] is that interactions with the technologies of transformation leave their marks no matter what; they reveal nature as a lie. Perhaps with more early transitioning, trans politics will come to resemble intersex politics more, with people wondering what their lives would have been like if they'd had a different history of embodiment. But then, who knows? It's a risky business to try to predict the future.

JJ: Human beings are social animals. We do take cues from one another, and we do spread memes. Transgender identity as contagion? The term "contagion" infects the question. I suspect the recent attention/visibility fuels a certain trendiness. Purely metaphysical interrogation of personal gender identity is a great trend. Everyone should do it. Easy access to technologies of physical transition coupled with trans-trendiness is a recipe for regret. (Young) people ought to be cautious about making permanent changes to their bodies. What may be positively life-changing for a transsexual may be ultimately devastating for a genderqueer. It would be hypocritical to pretend that the demographics have not shifted and that there isn't peer pressure among young questioning people to claim an identity. It's great that the technologies exist. They should be used where they will help, and there should be no pressure either towards or against transition. Some trans discourses are already mainstream.

Trans-ness per se does not "taunt the social order" nor need it. Possibly "transgender" does, as an identity category. Certainly, the more exotic identities can do so as part of a (political) practice. I am personally dubious of a lot of identity politics, trans and otherwise. I prefer the quirkiness of individuals to movements and -isms.

CLB: Where do we go from here? Where do you see the future of trans discourse, as well as its method of delivery, going from here, beyond YouTube, Facebook, Tumblr, etc.?

JJ: Who are "we"? We are no more monolithic than any other general category of human. There are certainly trends in trans or any other discourse, but there is also a lot of diversity of opinion, POV, etc. That is a good thing, and I hope it will become more obvious and apparent and taken for granted. I do not want a unified front; strength and unity in numbers is the foundation of fascist thought, and totalitarianism can approach from the right or the left. We will use whatever delivery method is trending at any given time . . . maybe real-time, holographic, sensory-enhanced chat?

III. Fear of a Trans Planet

"The availability of intervention and the outspokenness of the transgender community *are causing* a lot more people to see themselves as transgender, and at younger ages," Alice Dreger, a bioethicist, ominously declares in "About a Boy."[12]

Human interest stories about transgender folks often employ an expert like Dreger in such a manner, as a supposedly objective voice of logical and calm scientific authority to whom we, the readers, can turn to for assurance, someone whose voice may be trusted. Can we go on listening to this transgender person's lived experience(s), told in their own words, without looking back over our shoulder for that paternalistic voice of the expert who keeps us on the correct path of understanding? Stories such as "About a Boy," which on the surface seem to be positive and affirming of transgender individuals, still place the real narrative power of transgender lives in the words of those who represent centers of power in medical, mental health, and legal discourses.

The article's author, Margaret Talbot, profiles a young female-to-male transgender boy named Skylar. We are taken into a liberal, affluent world where parents want to do anything—*anything*—to help their children to be happy and successful, including allowing them to transition from one gender to another at the age of sixteen. There has been a rising trend in recent years of people self-identifying as transgender at younger and younger ages. Early in the article, Talbot posits the cause of this phenomenon is largely due to the vociferousness and organization of trans activists. She points to a study which finds that the younger a transgender person is, "the more likely they were to have had 'access to transgender people at a young age.'"[13] The negative space around this matter of access is the implication of *transgender wrongness*. Young people exposed to transgender people risk "seeing" themselves as transgender also. The "cause" of this phenomena, the article implies, must be sniffed out. The onus is on transgender people, who, by exposing their existence to others, lead unsuspecting young people to "become" trans.

Non-normative gender identity is implied to be a contagion, a thing that people can pass from one to another; and perhaps like a disease, one can imagine avoiding exposure. This echoing negative space also misses the more interesting and important question: What is it that causes any of us to come to "see" ourselves as *any* variegation of gender in the first place? It is inaccurate to say there are two kinds of genders: normative ones and everyone else. Discourse from regimes of power which attempt to sift out the "cause" of non-normative genders, bodies, and sexualities inherently raise my suspicion—I fear the questions following the "whys and hows" will be questions of how such divergence from the sense dominant norms can then be eradicated, purged, quieted, stopped, extinguished. Allies of non-gender-normative people who want to determine the "cause" of how people become non-normative in bodies, genders, and sexualities may do their work with far better intentions, but when the conversation veers toward essentialism, and risks reinforcing notions of "real" and inauthentic, natural vs. constructed, sorting out who is inherently trans, inherently queer, and who is not, I take objection. I'm not the only one who remembers the discovery of "the gay gene" in the late 1990s, am I?

When the power of transgender discourse is decentralized, the "subjugated knowledges" of the trans experience rise to the surface, and polyvalent identities are able to be expressed, shared, and heard, the control of these centers of power over our bodies is diminished. The trans person can reject pathology and join the ranks of diverse forms of human existence. The lived narrative no longer needs to be subjugated beneath the story the medical/psycho/juridical discourse has crafted as ours. Eva Hayward speaks to this need for the bodily knowledge of trans lives to be heard:

> The personal is not the same as the individual but an opportunity to see how lived experience is the basis for investigation of more generalizable forms (Sobchack 2006). By redeploying the medicalized legacy of transsexuals self-narrativizing, constructing a diachronic of narrative from a synchronous field of wrong body-ness so that a diagnosis can be given, I use my own carnal knowledge of transsexuality to push back at larger political, historical, and cultural currents. Rather than reading such reflexivity as navel-gazing or as a failure of critical distance, I want to say that transsexuality is necessarily predicated on kinds of self-disclosure and as such the bodily feel of transitioning is unavoidably "personal."[14]

Self-disclosure was the project of the youth who included me on that Facebook trans-coming-out announcement.

Skylar, the boy written about in *The New Yorker*, who transitioned to male at sixteen, also sees the big picture with calm nonchalance: "Every person has their own gender and will deal with it the way they deal with it." But Talbot still has an audience to reassure in *The New Yorker's* readership, and she tells us that even if a young person hasn't met a real live trans person in the flesh, one might become *exposed* to trans people, nevertheless. Mainstream media has increasingly made references to transgender people and have had transgender characters on programs. These days, more positive representations of trans characters might be seen on programs like *Glee* or *30 Rock*, where in past decades any rare trans characters in mainstream entertainment could only be portrayed as desperate, disempowered "street-walkers" or serial killers—or both. Just today, as I was writing this, I heard "Click and Clack, the Tappet Brothers" on the popular public radio program "Car Talk" made an FTM/trans man joke: "our transgender studies expert: *Ben Hur.*" Not a hilarious joke, but not particularly offensive, either, I noted, or, at least not to me.

Talbot rightly mentions the profusion of transgender content on to be found on the Internet: Young people today post transition pictures on Facebook, updates on Twitter and Tumblr. Countless YouTube videos document everything trans-related: from practical, hands-on content such as hormone self-injection tutorials and voice lessons; to personal diary videos that intimately detail the emotional and physical experiences of transition; to videos that ruminate on more self-absorbed minutiae of the process, where a single chin hair is examined and discussed as if it is the very beard of Paul Bunyan. Second puberties are dissected as intensely as first puberties are endured. Talbot mentions We Happy Trans, a site where positive stories of trans people are posted by trans people, featuring a cornucopia of young people describing their experiences.

A social worker named Logan, who provides services for disenfranchised and at-risk transgender youth at Larkin Street in San Francisco (youth who would likely have a very different experience around expressing their gender identities than Skylar) acknowledges the impact the Internet has made on transgender language: "If you look back ten years ago, every queer organization was 'L.G.B.' Then a couple years later it was: 'L.G.B.T.' But then gender identity started changing and varying, and those communities started becoming more visible, and the definitions that people were using and youth were using, all this was changing what generations were cycling through, specifically with the Internet. So we saw the use of genderqueer, gender-variant, and two-spirited, and all this stuff. And so as a provider you have to constantly have those conversations to know what the language is and what people are comfortable with."[15] Logan gives insight into the manner in which the way trans people talk about themselves is in turn informing service-agency discourse.

Today, one can drop the word "transgender" into Google and bring up 56,100,000 results in *twenty seconds*.[16] As Eve Shapiro points out, the Internet "functions both as a tool for activists and as a space within which activism can happen."[17] The anxious undercurrent of Talbot's article is a fear that the voices of transgender people are running wild, an unregulated dialouge with unprecedented reach. People who are troubled by a belief that the outspokenness of marginalized communities recruits others to join the ranks of such populations *should* worry—transgender people are talking to others, and each other, at a rate that was unimaginable only a decade ago and virtually impossible two decades ago. Shapiro contends that, "There has been a shift in the transgender community from a pathologized transsexual population that existed around support and informational groups to a politicized transgender community that challenges society's gender paradigms."[18] The current state of discourse about transgender people is increasingly authored by trans people for other trans people and trans allies, and the usual arbiters of such discourses—doctors and surgeons, psychiatrists and therapists; and juridical officials of all ranks (outside of transgender people who do work in these occupations, of course)—have no active voice in these discourses. But Shapiro cautions us to remember that, "Because the Internet creates a space in which a large number of trans people can congregate without having to face, directly, the social stigma and attendant consequences of being trans, the Internet can foster a false sense of security and an inflated sense of social change and acceptance."[19]

Despite the prudent reminder that Shapiro offers, we can see a shift from a trans discourse issued from outside, toward a decentralized, multi-voiced discourse of which, as Susan Stryker suggests, the medical, mental health, and legal voices are only but a part of.

"Within systems of thought which have a vested interest in ignoring the inescapable fact that even the most global analysis is tied to the particular (raced, sexed, classed, educated) body of the analyst who conceives it (because not to do so would unmask its enabling privileges), no place is shunted to the periphery of consideration with greater alacrity than is the body," she writes in "Dungeon Intimacies." Perhaps for the first time in history, the experiential knowledge of trans lives, bodies, and minds—organized, researched, shared, and articulated *by trans people for trans people*—have allowed trans voices to emerge from the shadows of power that have historically controlled both actual trans lives and trans narratives. As Skylar tells Talbot, "'The Internet, and the fact that there are resources readily available,' had made a big difference in his decision to change gender. 'That makes it much easier for ideas to spread . . . and this is just another idea to be spread.'"[20]

Notes

1. Susan Stryker, "Dungeon Intimacies: The Poetics of Transsexual Sadomasochism," *Parallax* 14, no. 1 (2008): 7.

2. Alan Ellis, *The Harvey Milk Institute Guide to Lesbian, Gay, Bisexual, Transgender, and Queer Internet Research* (New York: Harrington Park Press, 2002), 68.

3. Ibid., 67.

4. Eve Shapiro, "Trans'cending Barriers: Transgender Organizing on the Internet," *Journal of Gay & Lesbian Social Services* 16 (2004), 165–179.

5. Susan Stryker, "(De)Subjugated Knowledges: An Introduction to Transgender Studies," *The Transgender Studies Reader*, eds. Susan Stryker and Stephen Whittle (New York: Routledge, 2006), 6.

6. Susan Stryker and Aren Z. Aizura, *The Transgender Studies Reader 2* (New York: Routledge, 2013).

7. I wrote an article, "Dungeon Intimacies," a few years back about that queer/trans moment in the early '90s. I even mention you in [the article].

8. World Professional Association for Transgender Health; formerly the Harry Benjamin International Gender Dysphoria Association.

9. Yahoo Groups essentially became defunct in October 2019.

10. Margaret Talbot, "About a Boy: Transgender Surgery for Teens," *New Yorker Magazine*, 2013, 56–65.

11. Susan Stryker, "My Words to Victor Frankenstein Above the Village of Chamounix: Performing Transgender Rage," *GLQ* 1, no. 3, 237–254.

12. Talbot, 2013.

13. Ibid.

14. Eva Hayward, "Spiderwomen: Notes on Transpositions," *Transgender Migrations: The Bodies, Borders, and Politics of Transition*, ed. Trystan Cotten (Hoboken: Taylor and Francis, 2012), 93.

15. Toby Eastman, *Larkin Street Stories: Working with Transgender Youth* (Rockville, MD: Homelessness Resource Center, Substance Abuse and Mental Health Services Administration, 2011).

16. As this book is about to go to print, that number is about 179,000,000 results in 0.79 seconds.

17. Shapiro, 2004.

18. Ibid., 166.

19. Ibid., 58.

20. Talbot, 2013.

Lessons from the Locker Room

Prior to transition, I was as active as I could have been given that I had no relationship to my body at all. I remember this instant sense of being in my body after my very first shot of T, perhaps psychosomatic, but I didn't care. After chest surgery, I developed adult-onset athleticism. Having a new relationship with my body, I felt eager to see what it could do. My body and I were like a brand-new couple, crackling with NRE, marveling at how even the mundane bits of life could feel so thrilling. I lifted weights three times a week, learned how to do handstands, began to train for a century race (a 100-mile road bike ride), hiked more often with my dogs, and joined a soccer team—and I hadn't played organized sports since my junior year of high school, when I got kicked off my team due to some failing grades and problems at home. I quit smoking, ate better, drank infrequently, and slept more. I became more athletic in my late thirties than I had ever been in my life because I could actually show up to be present in my body. Exercise, I discovered, improved my mental health.

Early in transition, no place evoked internal contention and palm-moistening anxiety like the locker room. Out in the world, I mostly enjoyed the blissful nobody-ness of being seen as a guy. After years of being freaked out-on in women's restrooms and having security called on me, it was a relief to be suddenly nondescript and virtually invisible.

But in the locker room, all bets are off.

AT FIRST, I changed at home whenever possible and showed up at the gym ready to work out. Eventually, I had to "sack up," as they say in the locker room, and deal—I didn't always have the luxury of suiting up into my kit at home before a session. But changing at the gym caused time to slow to a cold and glacial movement. I hurriedly fumbled with my shorts and jammed myself close to my locker, staring at the floor. Afterward, I found it difficult to make eye contact or engage with other guys in the weight room, as if they'd remember me as that awkward changer from the locker room.

The first time I entered the men's locker room at the local high-end spa where my then-girlfriend worked as a massage therapist (and where I could soak for free in the fancy tubs), I was bluntly watched by some of the other men. I cringed under their scrutiny, as validating as it might have been to my manhood to be cruised by gay men. I stripped down to my boxer briefs, put on my spa kimono, and, leaving it open, I moved in close to my locker, whipped off my boxers and packer, quickly stuffed them in a wad in my locker, and—once outside—slipped into the dark cloak of hot water. I had to laugh at myself when I observed guys in the tub with man boobs that rivaled my pre-surgery chest. Later, my buddy, a fellow trans man, reassured me, "Dude, you will never get stared at in another locker room the way you get stared at in the locker room at Ten Thousand Waves."

As I progressed in my transition, I began to see these locker room moments as a valuable education into the myriad ways of being a man in the world. I learned that it's not okay to talk to other guys in the locker room, except when it is: Generally, the other guy has to start speaking first. No one knows how the guy who initiates conversation knows that it is okay to do so, but he does. As a man of trans experience, the initiator likely will not be you.

Once, while getting dressed, I was approached by a completely naked (save for flip-flops) septuagenarian. Unabashed in his nudity, he said with a thick New York accent, "You have more keys on your belt than a Manhattan building superintendent!" Being a guy means not caring (nor showing you care) what anyone may think of you strutting your stuff—beer bellies, back hair, dickie-do's, muffin tops, man boobs, droopy ball sacks—across a locker room, a weight room, or the deck of an Olympic pool.

My confidence has increased with time. Now I change

right next to other guys in the locker room without a flinch. My new locker room challenge: I enrolled in a swimming class at the local community college, which brought the issue up a level. Now the challenge is to change into swim trunks, no briefs, no packer/jock strap configuration, and walk out into the pool area. I am self-conscious of not packing, of my chest scars being scrutinized. Good thing I am covered in tattoos—I consider it my dazzle camouflage, deflecting notice from my scars to the bright colors tracing all over my arms and torso.

Recently, after using a gang shower at the same time as another guy, he came over to the bench where I was dressing. He threaded a towel between his legs, one foot propped on a bench, and commenced to dry his boney white ass off about a foot away from my face while chatting with me about his wife and kids and the place we were both vacationing. Communal shower use is a locker room black belt move I'll likely not repeat soon. It made me wonder, though: *Are trans men the only ones taught not to talk to other guys in the locker room?*

The thing I have to remember is that in most situations, everyone is so absorbed with thinking about themselves that they likely are not paying much attention to me or you. And even if someone notices my scars, so what if they realize I'm trans? There are many ways to be a man: The locker room is proof of this.

Pigeon Hunters

Today a pigeon flew into the shop and pattered between the rafters with a lonesome and slow slapping of wings. *How could anything stay aloft being so calm and lazy?* The warehouse yawns open to ease the noxious cloud of our welding on this one project for six weeks, ten hours a day, six days a week. Welding, making metal part of other metal. We're four white guys, gray with soot, trying to get this damn job done on time.

When we open the big bay doors, any sort of riffraff tends to wander on in: homeless guys who rob the honor-system snack box for cash but leave the nasty orange crackers with peanut butter behind; a small Asian man with question-mark posture, holding up a watch or bars of soap or something else for sale; bicycle thieves; and, of course, pigeons.

The pigeons come in all nonchalant, heads bobbing on thick gunmetal necks. "Hey guys, where's the party? I like snacks. Coo. Coo!" And then they fly up through the cavernous building, soar to the rafters, wings flashing in tight corkscrew turns, and get confused, realizing, "Oh fuck, I'm stuck." Then they just find a spot on the rafters to rest and recoup. Those orange eyeballs scope out a new possible squat. Eventually someone notices our unwelcome guest.

"Pigeon! Up there! Get it! *Pigeon!*"

Nothing sparks workers' gleeful ire like a pigeon in the shop. Tools are dropped, welding helmets are tossed onto bench-tops, and everyone huddles together at a decent vantage point below. Even the foreman's pale Irish cheeks are flushed with color. This is a perfectly legitimate reason to bring all work to a grinding halt.

Gary runs to his locker and pulls out a pair of wrist-rockets, a type of lethal slingshot that was practically a felony to own where I grew up, south of Boston. My brother owned one when I was a kid, and it symbolized the unfair gender disparities of my childhood. My pocketknife was taken away from me for touching my uvula with the point of the blade, like a sideshow act, after shouting, "Watch this!" But my brother got to set the woods on fire and own a slingshot that could kill a kid.

Gary positions one slingshot over his forearm, inserts some 7/16" hex nuts into the soft suede pouch, pulls back on the thick elastic band, and with his weapon fully cocked, spins 180 degrees and says, "Where's the pigeon gone to, huh? Where is he?"

I GUESS it's the boredom. Days growing into each other with a vague memory of some moment of sleep in between; before you know it, bowl of cereal, coffee on the stove, dog walking and barking at you through dewy grass, sun trying to push through the thick spring fog of dawn, morning crows yelling at you, yelling at the dog, kiss your sweet sweetheart good-bye, and you're back again as if you'd never left. This is what you do, cutting metal apart and welding the parts together. I really need two days off in a row; I'm fucking bored by exhaustion.

I pick up Gary's other slingshot, grab some cupped, round pellets of steel off the concrete floor near the huge, blue Scotchman Ironworker punch, and follow him. The pigeon flutters from its perch to another a few feet away and glances around, head bobbing.

I load up some of the steel, punched-out pellets, pull back on the slingshot as far as I can, aim at the bird some twenty-five feet above, and let go. Metal bits ping and ricochet, feathers fan through the air, and the unharmed pigeon tucks itself into a tight spot between a rafter and the concrete apex of the wall. Gary and I aim again while other workers shout and cheer as they put on safety glasses and duck away.

Laughing, blood pushing through my lungs and cheeks, I aim and miss, aim and miss. It is exhilarating, hilarious. Nobody is working anymore in any part of the shop; everyone is completely involved in the hunting. Gary, a duck hunter, actually gets close to the bird a couple of times.

I am a pretty good shot, but find it impossible to locate my sights accurately between the aluminum arms of the slingshot.

Pigeons are not stupid. They are plentiful and reputed to be filthy, they proliferate extensively and are disliked, but they are not stupid. They have this tenacity that allows them to thrive in the filth at our human hem, even while we sully our own nest. This gray and purple pariah will outlast the best of us. Our quarry demonstrates this tenacious will to live by working himself into a crevice that we cannot shoot into from below.

"Roust him. Christ, get him to fly into me," Gary shouts, squinting through his slingshot. I picture him in olive drab hip waders, a shotgun broken open and resting like a cat across his forearm while he pushes serenely and silently through a marsh, then snaps into Rambo-readiness at the cut of feathers through air. *Shotgun snapping shut with purpose. BAM!*

"Fuck this." Gary throws his weapon down in disgust and turns to find better equipment. I make a couple more shots in the direction of the holed-up bird, but he doesn't even rustle his wings. I stop laughing and catch my breath. I toss my slingshot aside, snap up my greasy, tan leather sleeves, put my welding helmet back on, pull on my thick, gray leather gloves, and punch the ON button of the Miller. The machine purrs to life; the fan flutters inside the welder. I get the nozzle into position against the steel frame and with a sharp nod, I flick my helmet down over my face. Through the weld, I embark upon an existential crisis about what it means to take a life. *What do I care if a pigeon bumbles into our building? The worst that could happen, maybe the bird shits on a couple of machines, big friggin' deal.* The blue light flashes against me and I hide my sudden shame beneath the hood. I watch the thin blue arc of the weld puddle beneath the tip of the MIG nozzle. When I finish, I flip the hood back with a gloved thumb to find Tom, the lead painter, standing there in his shiny bald pate and immaculate, white work clothes, looking like a weird guru or maybe a lean Mr. Clean. *How does he keep his clothes so damn spotless, especially here?*

"I was pretty surprised to look over and see *you* running around shooting at a bird. I mean, you looked all *happy.*" Tom nods at his own words, like he's reading my mind. "Yeah, like, once, when I was kid, we'd get all excited throwing things at people, and then once I actually hit a kid in the head and I felt like an *asshole.*" Tom's eyes are wide-open as he speaks.

I nod, thinking of times I've felt this same overwhelming rush of adrenaline mixed with naughtiness, coated with lung-aching laughter, followed by a bitter mouthful of crow. The slideshow of memory feels random. It begins with me, age eight, stalking through my neighbors' mossy backyard with a bow and arrows I'd constructed from elderberry branches, stalking cottontail rabbits. I was a child survivalist. I'd always sensed the shit would hit the fan someday, and when it did, I planned to live. Learning to hunt seemed logical.

I came across no rabbits that day, but the next time I saw baby rabbits blinking their innocent black eyes and nibbling clover in our back yard, I felt like a monster to have considered killing one of them. The endpoint of hunting suddenly struck me: It meant *to kill*—something I hadn't at that point thought all the way through to its inevitable conclusion.

Just a few years afterward, I found a spear, a small metal trident fitted to the end of a wooden pole, sticking out of a neighbor's trash can. Raised by my mother to be a complete scavenger, I rode home on my bike in triumph with it clutched in one hand, dangling by my side like a jousting lance. It was summertime and I brought the spear when I went snorkeling in the brisk water of Cape Cod. I loved being underwater; it was the only place I could find quiet. While I floated along silently, I made out the faintest outlines of a flounder camouflaged in the sand.

I plunged my spear down into it and sprung up out of the water, triumphant. But the water had magnified the writhing, flat fish, and once out of it, the flounder seemed pathetic and small. I panicked. My father's rule about fishing was that we had to eat whatever we caught and kept. I thought of how he would say that the fish was too small, his voice heavy with disappointment and annoyance—anger, maybe. I frantically wrested the fish from the trident, yanking its body back over the barbed points, its blood flowing out, watered down by the sea. I pushed the fish back into the water, but it was too torn up; it was too late. The fish floated slowly away from me on the current, belly up.

The shame crescendo was seventh grade gym class. I was a kid who never fit in and was often harassed, teased, or heckled, until I became a freshman and would swear crazily at anyone who fucked with me until they got frightened and left me alone. There were kids who were fucked with *a lot* more than I was, relentlessly so. Mary McFeely was one of these kids. Mary was so acutely shy that if you even spoke to her, her soft, pale cheeks would rise up crimson-red and she would turn away. Mary McFeely hurt no one, bothered no one, offended no one—she took up *no* space. For this she was harangued by packs of relentless, pretty, well-adjusted, socially thriving girls. One day after a drive-by of insults, I was lured in by the momentary seduction of the pack—as if they'd ever include me—and I launched a verbal salvo at Mary McFeely. Her glistening, sad eyes held mine for a moment, and then she flushed and turned away while the popular girls snickered; for the moment, I was out of their range. One of them sent a basketball ricocheting by Mary's toes. A couple of minutes later, I saw tears streaking Mary's face.

I rushed over to her in the bleachers and said, "I'm sorry Mary, I'm really sorry." It was too late. I saw in Mary's eyes that I was just like the rest of them: cruel and longing to crush anything soft.

After lunch break, the foreman and Gary are giggling and putting an air-nozzle up to a long piece of galvanized pipe. The foreman fashions darts out of lengths of copper welding rod with masking tape flights. He loads them into the pipe, and Gary pulls the trigger on the air nozzle.

"I get off on killing birds," Gary announces with a sweet grin on his face. The darts fly up softly, touch the concrete wall a yard below the pigeon, and fall away, swiveling back down to the floor like spiny flowers falling from a tree in bloom.

"Wait, I got it," shouts the foreman, brandishing a sixteen-penny nail gun and laughing like a boy. He attaches the nail gun to an air hose and pushes the tip of it into the pipe, which releases the safety mechanism. Gary aims the pipe, and the foreman pulls the trigger, and with a loud *ssshhoounk*, sixteen-penny nails fire from the pipe, sparking when they hit the iron rafters, sticking into the wooden ceiling or bouncing back and careening dangerously down toward all of us below.

The ruckus startles the pigeon, who springs forth and is struck in the body at least once. The bird walks out into the open along a rafter, is pelted again, and turns on heel and waddles quickly back toward his little nook but is struck again by another nail. He moves like an old-fashioned arcade duck, like a red and white bullseye might pop up on his chest. But he flaps over to another rafter a dozen feet away.

Gary likes punk rock and country music, same as me. We've maintained a totalitarian hold on the radio station selection and keep it on college airwaves. He is affable and smart. He is kind to most people and reserves his razor wit for those who deserve it. He has a cultured passion for beer and can describe beers like a five-star waiter. He is quite well-versed in the minutiae of queer culture, but isn't showy or lecherous about it. Of all the guys in the shop, I like Gary best. Years before, I'd asked Gary if I could go duck hunting with him. I told him I wasn't really interested in shooting any birds, I just wanted to hang out and shoot guns. He really tried to not wrinkle his nose at me. He just squinted through his glasses and didn't say anything, which meant *no*. No, he would not take a non-hunter hunting.

"FUCK THIS." Gary drops his weapon, while the foreman and another welder, Lucas, swap hunting tales. Lucas is so in the moment that he shakes out a pack of Marlboros and lights one with the flint striker that hangs from his heavy work pants by a lanyard of greasy suede, even though he's standing beside a tall tank of flammable acetylene. Gary marches up to the shop's open mezzanine level, only ten feet below the rafters now, with a 3/8" crown staple gun in his hand. He hooks it up to an air-hose, holds back the safety with his fingers, and machine-guns thumb-long staples at the bird. It's difficult to see either of them, but the shooting and raining down of spent staples is cacophonous. A couple of times I think I hear the thud of metal against hollow bird bones, the snapping of feathers.

"Die! Just fucking *die!*" Gary shouts. I see sweat running clean lines down through the metal soot on his face. He's hoisting the heavy staple gun straight above his head in one hand like it's a pistol, shaking it in the direction of the tattered pigeon.

"I've hit you so many times—*why won't you die!*" Real frustration scratches Gary's voice.

He comes back down, wipes his face with a rag, and suits up into his leathers again. He's silent, and when he crowns himself with his filthy welding helmet it is understood that he is, at least for the time being, conceding. Everyone else has long since lost interest. I look up to the bird above. It hasn't moved, but it's still alive, high up on a rusty beam. The primary feathers of one wing hang low and useless.

Gary flips back his helmet with a blackened glove.

"I'm mad. I'm too overstimulated to even attempt to get any work done." His cola-brown eyes glower over his grimy face.

I've abandoned the hunt—later, Gary will call me a pussy. Pigeons are flying rats and deserve to die, so advocating mercy for them is like asking my co-workers to feed their kids lollipops they found stuck to a movie theater floor. I swish the idea around and through my mind like mouthwash, but I find no way in which the death of this bird gains me anything.

"This is fucking depressing," I say. "Just kill it and put an end to it."

"I *am* gonna kill it," Gary says. "Soon."

"Yeah, I can just picture this bird flying around, arrows sticking out of it everywhere, and you caught up in it, tied to its side, one arm flapping in the breeze. *Argg, we are hunting the Great Gray Bird…*" I laugh at my mental image: Gary with an Ahab beard.

He doesn't laugh along with me.

"I'm gonna get that bastard tomorrow."

IN THIS world of machines and men—men who work so hard and fuck with each other even harder—holding onto a sense of compassion required a tremendous amount of resolve. I constantly teetered on a fulcrum. In the shop, on the job, in the union hall, I occupied a liminal and ever-shifting locus of being regarded as both masculine, even manly, and yet—still *only* a woman. And in the entire rest of my life, women were *everything*. I loved arriving at the Lexington Club on my motorcycle on Friday nights after a long week in the shop in grime-blackened Carhartts and steel-toed boots, ready to drink away my exhaustion and cruise the beautiful queer women of the Mission.

On the precipice of my decision to transition, a choice that came slowly and in fragments, I was an anthropologist studying masculinity, trying to figure out what to take on as my own and what to discard. I was simultaneously one of the guys, a butch, an outcast, a shapeshifter, and someone that could be counted on to get shit done. I wanted to get along, move through long work hours with ease—have camaraderie, if not a work-friendship with the others. When I wanted to learn something new and more technically complicated, that was regarded as stepping out of line. But then I was one of the stronger backs and set of biceps relied upon to load the truck, and I was always depended upon to take on responsibility. Some days this job provided me with more masculine fulfillment than my skeleton could bear. Other days it was *Lord of the Flies* in the warehouse. *Put down the conch shell, boys!*

The day the union guy came in to organize our shop, it was like looking into the clean face of Jesus and knowing we'd be saved. The remote island of the shop had been officially visited by an adult who'd hopefully put an end to the barbarism of its culture. I'd traded three backbreaking cooking jobs for this one backbreaking job in the shop. I'd have to exercise hypervigilance against the gravitational flow into giving up and succumbing to the idea that this was as good as life could be.

GARY AND Lucas bring pellet guns to work the next morning. They load fresh CO_2 cartridges and pack the guns to capacity with pellets. On coffee break, Lucas chucks scraps of 2x4s into the rafters to try to get the staunch, still-alive pigeon to move. It won't.

Lucas and Gary swear a colorful tapestry of obscenity and anger. They take turns popping off shots from the air pistols, but the damned bird will not budge.

The air is even more ominous than the day before. Ugly. I skip lunch and work on a personal project, a wooden toolbox, something to funnel my anxiety into. The guys come back from lunch early, and since they have guns and the pigeon will not oblige them by coming out of hiding, they take turns shooting them across the warehouse at a Coke can propped up on the drill press. I look up from the workbench to watch the guys popping off shots and missing.

I can't take it. I put down my square and the pin-nailer. I walk over to Gary and Lucas and hold my palm out. Lucas places the air pistol into my hand. I point the gun out at arm's length, find the Coke can through the sights and squeeze off a round. The shot hits the can with a loud, satisfying *plink*.

As the can falls to the ground, I hand back the gun and mutter, "Assholes."

Splinters

The worst of the summer crunch is over. I milk menial tasks all day, hide in the cool, dark theater basement sending dirty texts, sneak a nap in the seat of the forklift, and write stories in my notebook. For us year-round carpenters, the crescendo builds to opening day of the opera season, and then we try to do as little as possible for forty hours a week until the end of August and the summer stock. My busywork for today is to clean up the backstage deck overlooking the pinon tree-pocked mountains between here and Los Alamos, dispatching rusty debris from welding projects, old hardware, and cracked and abandoned staging to our dumpster, or to a trailer we will empty at the Santa Fe dump.

I grab a wooden platform that's been baking in the sun. The black paint is coming up in scales. It's heavier than I expect. As I pull to lift it, I feel an ugly, sliding pinch in the palm of my hand. I freeze, knowing. I look; it's worse than I expect.

A black sliver of plywood is buried deep, about four inches long, an eighth of an inch wide. More than half is stuck in the heel of my right palm. The pointed end of the splinter presses against my flesh from the inside, making the skin protrude but not puncturing all the way through. It's so deep the black wood disappears from view inside my skin.

I try to pull it out with my fingers, but the splinter does not budge. Pounding pain travels down my forearm, louder and louder. My palm is swelling, turning red around the spear of wood. I bite the end of the splinter, trying to wrest it free with my teeth. It doesn't move, but the external part of the splinter snaps off, leaving the rest lodged. I retrieve the tweezers from the metal first aid box mounted on the shop wall. I wipe them clean with an alcohol pad, then approach my boss, the master carpenter, whom I cannot stand. He's a complete dick, but he's also a volunteer firefighter. I assume he has some medical ability, so I thrust my hand heel-forward to him, my fingers curled in.

"Can you help me," I say, matter-of-fact.

His thick mustache twitches at me, annoyed. He looks down at my hand and squints.

"Oh, wow." He sounds genuinely impressed.

"Can you pull it out?"

He forgets he hates me too and shakes his head. "Nope. You're going to the clinic."

I'm excited; I get to leave work, get out of the blazing sun and into an air-conditioned room, probably get a vial

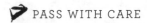 PASS WITH CARE

of painkillers—these occupational clinics love to dole out the narcotics. Another carpenter drives me to the workers' comp clinic.

The doctor takes one look at my hand. "Jesus Christ!" She tosses her hands up, as if exasperated. "And it's *painted*, too. Shit!"

"Just trying to keep things interesting. I know you're sick of sprained ankles."

Every summer, the opera absorbs hundreds of college theater apprentices for the season, and we try to break as many of them as possible. This summer so far, there's been 112 summer workplace injuries. I am injury number 113.

I sit on the medical table, legs dangling. The doc tells me she's going to have to cut the splinter out. I nod. I chat with her and the receptionist and make jokes: my survival tactic. She cleans my hand. Pain dances up my neck and forehead. I watch with deep interest as she slices open my palm with a scalpel. The skin parts like a sigh and I'm still watching, fascinated—when suddenly I feel very hot and I'm dreaming that I'm in Manhattan, walking down a crowded sidewalk and everyone passing me says my name over and over again.

Next thing, I'm lying on the examination table with a cold, wet cloth on my forehead, soaked in sweat. My hand is swaddled in an enormous bandage. The doctor laughs.

"I passed out?"

She nods and shakes a plastic vial, making a high rattle. My splinter, saved like a relic of the cross.

I HAVE a penchant for fucked-up splinters. Last time, I was freelancing, doing a carpentry project in my friend Beth's studio. I got a splinter deep in my right index finger. I tried to pull it out with no luck, and showed it to Beth, who shivered and looked away. "We gotta take you to the hospital."

"No, I don't have health insurance."

I pulled my Leatherman from its belt-sheath and tried to pluck the splinter. It was stuck in the meat of the muscle—so much that I couldn't bend my finger.

"Try it, just yank."

"No." Beth was horrified. "I'm gonna puke."

"I can't afford the hospital. I can't deal with registering for indigent-status at the emergency room. It'll take for-ever—this hurts!"

I thought of Killian, who fucked up her ankle roller skating. Another friend, a vet tech, snuck her into the animal hospital at night and took an X-ray. Luckily, her ankle wasn't broken. I got an idea.

"Let's go to Holy Holes!" Holy Holes was our friend Calliope's piercing and tattoo studio. "Dude, that place is cleaner than the hospital, and they have scalpels and for-ceps. Besides, Calliope will *love* it!"

Calliope positively reveled in the yucky and perverse. She was an undertaker by trade, and often said without irony that she was on her last life, according to her astrological sign. Blood and guts were of the corporeal world, which she was finished with; she was unflapped by any aspect of the human body. She was thrilled when I presented my swollen, impaled finger to her.

"Oooh. Lovely," she crooned, then whisked me into a piercing room, sat me on an ancient barber chair, rustled through the vintage medical cabinets and pulled out cotton swabs, gauze pads, iodine, green soap, forceps, a scalpel, and bandages. She tried to attach forceps onto the protruding nub of lumber in my finger. My whole body jolted.

"Want a Valium?" she asked. I nodded as she reached into her purse. She put on latex gloves and tried again to wrestle my splinter. It wouldn't budge. The doorbells jangled and she left me to attend to a customer. The Valium kicked in. I giggled, even though it killed.

"I'm gonna have to cut you open a little, okay?" Calliope said as she swept back into the room.

"Fun. Are you psyched?"

"Mm-hmm." She bent her head over my finger and sliced. I swallowed a groan.

For two hours, Calliope and Wilton, another piercer, took turns trying to get a bite on the splinter in between piercing navels and eyebrows. Other friends came by the shop—Matty and Jen gave it a try, too. In pain delirium, I gave it a go when Calliope left to pierce a nipple. I managed to clamp the forceps down on the splinter and clicked them shut. "Wilton, Wilton!" He came running in with Beth, who'd stayed out of the room, feeling ill.

"Look, I got it . . . pull the fucker out. Pull it." He yanked. It didn't move. I howled. "Harder."

He pulled again, heaving his big shoulders back, and I felt it pull free, my own little Excalibur. Blood gushed. Calliope bandaged me up and kissed me on the lips.

"All better."

I READ about a bowhead whale caught near Alaska by Inupiat fishermen. They found a piece of 130-year-old harpoon stuck in the whale's flesh. Imagine carrying around something so old and painful inside of you for so long. My friend Kris had cancer everywhere in her body—she told me she knew it was because of the way she metabolized anger. She didn't die of cancer, she died of suicide. She wanted the choice before the cancer took that away, too.

I've held so much anger inside of myself. And sadness. When I was younger, I walked through my days spraying sadness like a shotgun blast. As an artist, it was allowed—even expected—to explode in front of everyone, creating and destroying in fits and bursts. Some called me angry. They judged. Some people saw that I carried something thick and cancerous inside of me and stuck their darkness inside me too, a bull with broken lances riddling my back and ribs. Plenty of people cannot carry their own darkness—they try to sneak it onto your back. They didn't understand that the splinters tearing through me were just grief, sickness, and loss. For what exploded out of me I buried ten times deeper inside my skin, all swole-up and festering.

I went out into the desert alone, and by the light of the waning moon I pulled each splinter free. Lightning struck the forests and the dry, crackling flames engulfed the mountains, who were begging to burn. Ponderosa pines love fire; it's like sex for the trees, the propagation of a species catalyzed by heat, but people are afraid. The fire threatened towns and the opera and the national laboratory—all the bullshit, the collected hate of the human race with a half-life of 100,000 years buried in steel drums under tarpaulins. The Christians call it rapture, but they too woke up at home, feeling angry, abandoned. Ash peppered down on Santa Fe. People kept a packed bag next to their front doors. Can you outrun burning hatred? Festering anger? It is a cleansing fire, a destruction to fertilize creation. I cried to the cholla, the sage, and the lonely, sad coyotes yipping in the night. I dropped my splinters on the thirsty ground. I still feel the scars. They hurt sometimes, but I am free. I am free.

Manhood Is Boring

The New Mexico wind in springtime is miserable, oppressive, sometimes even crazy-making, like a terrible voice of the id, standing on your shoulder and egging you on toward bad decisions. In the Galisteo Basin, the spring winds begin to howl through this desert bowl as early as February.

The construction site I am working on is in Eldorado, a massive subdivision east of Santa Fe that a mestizo friend of mine calls "the White Man's Reservation." The wind whips at us all day, yanking sheets of tar roofing paper from our hands or pulling out string lines that mark out the foundation. Carrying a full 4x8 sheet of sheathing plywood contorts you into a windsurfer on dry land. The wind trumpets into the auricle of your ears. Mine have only ever been so previously abused at a Mötorhead concert. At the end of my workday, I shut myself into my truck for the fifteen-mile-drive home, and the absence of wind roars thin white noise in my head.

Don tells me the locals' joke about why New Mexico is so

windy: "Because Arizona blows and Texas sucks." He coughs, then spits a loogie over his right shoulder, which hits the dust with a juicy smack. We are digging a sewer pipe ditch for an 800-square-foot home addition. New Mexico soil is resistant to digging—rocky, hardened, and dry. The ditch starts out a couple feet deep near the addition and deepens to six feet when it connects to the house's existing exterior plumbing lines. I haven't measured the ditch, but my guess is that it must be thirty or forty yards long, and Don and I have the blisters-turned-callouses to prove it. It feels idiotic to dig a trench this long.

We mention this to our boss, Kristaps, a seventy-two-year-old Latvian dude whose family fled the Nazis when he was a small child. He used to work for NASA, so Don and I often say, "It ain't rocket science, Kristaps!" He mutters something about having worked for their atmospherics division, *not* their aeronautics programs.

Kristaps is like a worldly grandpa figure to me, a grandpa who rides a BMW motorcycle. But sometimes I catch myself watching him as he swings a pickaxe into the impenetrable caliche of high desert soil, thinking to myself, *Please goddess, don't let me be swinging a pickaxe at that age for a paycheck.*

Don stops pecking at the hardpan soil at the edge of the ditch with a heavy steel digging bar. He stoops and rests his chin on top of the bar. I am three feet below in the ditch, scooping out the soil he loosens with a spade. He stares down at me with a thoughtful, almost dreamy, expression. Don is tall, six-three maybe, thick, dark hair frosted with gray, arms covered with comic book tattoos: Batman leaps across a hairy forearm, Underdog demurs above an inner wrist, the Human Torch blazes up a defined triceps, and Wonder Woman stands, like noble cheesecake, with arms akimbo along the bulge of his bicep. His two front teeth protrude below his upper lip and rest, pressed into his full lower lip, two clicks on the dial from handsome toward goofy.

"So," he says, in his thick, born-and-raised Brooklyn accent, "am I supposed to call you *he* now?"

My shovel hits a rock and makes an uncomfortable sound, not unlike that of a fork skidding across a ceramic plate. I look up at Don from beneath the bill of my sweaty baseball cap. His expression is benign, open.

It seems that the wind holds its breath along with me. When I exhale, the incessant wind flaps like a tarp across my ears. Don is still waiting for my answer, not in any hurry to get back to digging. He was a Golden Gloves champ in his younger days, and he likes to go hide off behind a scraggly juniper to smoke a bowl, and comes back to work after swinging a few shadow punches into the howling wind. I poke at the bottom of the ditch with the tip of my shovel.

"Yeah," I say, "call me *he* now. That would be cool."

Don nods and drops the heavy digging bar down into the dirt. He pries loose a slice of reluctant earth. Spider-Man slings a web on Don's arm.

"So, are you gonna get a phalloplasty?"

He scans my face, my arched, questioning eyebrows.

"Dude, you'd be surprised what people like me learn about people like *you* from watching the Discovery Channel."

IN 2002, New Mexico was not exactly a hotbed of transgender awareness or resource. In the starkness of the high desert, you find out what you're made of. The desert is a landscape that neither coddles nor nurtures. It bleaches you down to your psychic bones and demands that you rebuild yourself from the dirt-up. I didn't exactly think through what it would mean to start my transition there.

I took my first shot of T in San Francisco that June, and the next day, I drove a pickup truck I'd purchased for $400 into the quiet, away from my known life, to figure out what the hell all of this meant. Santa Fe boasts a large queer community, but there isn't acceptance there like you might find in the major coastal cities. It's more like a "You don't fuck with me and I won't fuck with you" acceptance. A "don't ask, don't tell" acceptance. The blade of colonization still cuts deep in New Mexico, and its effects permeate life for Anglo, Indigenous, Hispanic, and Latinx people daily.

I experienced discrimination sometimes—for instance, at a local medical clinic (one I chose because I knew the staff had received a "trans 101" training), when I came down with a wracking, rib-cracking cough one winter. It took me three visits before I understood what was happening. The doctor treated me like I was being reckless with my health for taking testosterone and refused to address my serious respiratory ailment. As I began to change physically, I incurred suspicion from some queer women in the community; in their eyes, I was clearly a traitor.

But more often, I was happily surprised by the kindness with which I was treated. Don and Kristaps didn't care what pronoun I used, so long as I showed up for work, lifted heavy objects, and didn't complain about the incessant wind.

AT THE Santa Fe Unitarian Universalist Congregation, I sit in a multifunction room that smells like similar rooms in houses of worship everywhere: olfactory layers of weak coffee percolating in a large urn, dusty religious tomes, lacquered wood, and long-gone mothballs. Bright afternoon sunlight glances sharp and white through the clerestory windows, directly into my eyes and the eyes of the six other people sitting beside me.

We're a group of panelists, assembled here to answer questions about the LGBTQ community. For the last two weeks, members of the church could write any questions they might have for us and place their anonymous, folded slips of paper into a Folger's coffee can with a slit in the lid. They were invited to ask anything—no question too silly, the dumbest question is the one not asked, etc.

There are two young gay men, a couple. I've met them before. They are radiant, cute, with a similar height and build. They share the same wardrobe interchangeably. There are two elderly lesbians who have been together for fifty years. They both have soft, fluffy white hair and serene smiles. But for one of them, Alice, this serenity and white hair is a ruse to hide her dirty sense of humor and shameless flirting with anyone she chooses to make blush in the moment. There is a middle-aged, heterosexual, polyamorous couple—a man and a woman who are primary partners but will engage in secondary and tertiary relations with folks of any gender. I am thrilled to learn of their existence in sleepy old Santa Fe, a place that sometimes feels devoid of sexuality sometimes, especially after my extended tenure in anything-goes San Francisco. As "the" trans person, I am the only one not in a pair in this sexual/gender-minority Noah's Ark. Mary, the church member who asked us to come, hands us our questions, pre-sorted into identity-specific piles. My pile is the smallest.

We are introduced by name and by the topic of our little piles of questions. We smile awkwardly at one another as we are being introduced, like queer superfriends circling up for the first time as our unique powers are explained to each other. We take turns reading off our questions and doing our best to answer them.

"Does the Internet change how gay people meet each other?"

"Can lesbian couples legally adopt in New Mexico?"

"What exactly *can* you do in a polyamorous relationship?"
We all scootch to the edges of our folding chairs, eager to hear

the poly couple explain this. By the time the man has finished speaking, I am overwhelmed, perhaps even enlightened, by his utopian view of the human capacity for love, and pretty much convinced that default monogamy is a potential death sentence to the longevity of intimate connection.

A question to me: "What kinds of surgeries will you get?"

I answer, "Well, there are many different procedures available to trans men and trans women. Not all trans people choose to have surgery, because of existing health issues, cost, or quality of results, or because surgery may not be necessary for an individual to have a good quality of life."

A gray-haired woman in the front row pipes up. "But what about *you*?" She wags a finger from my knees to clavicles and back.

This is a question I get a lot—a well-intentioned but misplaced need to know about my private parts. "Well," I pause to emphasize a teachable moment, "if you wanna know what I look like naked, you could at least ask me out to dinner first." There is a long beat of silence and then the entire place erupts in laughter.

The Unitarian Universalists are a pretty informed and respectful bunch. This makes sense; the UU's have a program called OWLs, or Our Whole Lives, a comprehensive human sexuality education program for all church members in age-appropriate levels for everyone, children to senior citizens. I spoke to the OWLs cadre of thirteen-year-olds earlier in the year. Basically, it was the teacher and I having a conversation about transgender stuff while the early teens stared on in forced boredom. I was like a unicorn on display, except *who cares*? Even the kindest thirteen-year-old has a societal duty to be underwhelmed.

I read the last of my three questions, drawn in delicate, perfect longhand, clearly posed by one of the very old members of the church.

It asks, "What is the lifestyle of a transgender?"

FOR ALMOST thirty-three years, I bounced around in life from event to event, awash in trauma, allowing actions and reactions to those actions to steer the course of my life. I imagined that I would never survive my twenties, and when I did, I had no idea how to proceed. I had not actually decided that I would be here, that I would stick around and do this thing: live. At this point in my process, I now moved through life as a man.

After years of living adrift, I was finally steering my ship. Having made a choice, I was obsessed with figuring out what other choices I could make. Suddenly, it seemed like I couldn't stop making decisions. How do you explain all of that to a room full of strangers and the LGBTQI2S-plus-plus superfriends?

I LOOK at the expectant eyes watching me.

"Well, I can only speak for myself," I say, "but my life-style is basically this: I spend time with my girlfriend, go to work, cook food, make art and work on writing, putz in my garden, go hiking with my dogs, and work out at the gym."

Hearing myself, I am surprised by how regular—maybe even *boring*—my life has become. This had been the big fear. When I first divulged that I thought I might be trans to my radical, badass dyke friends back in mid-1990s San Francisco, a recurrent theme emerged: *We're kings and queens in a queer Shangri-La, a veritable Neverland of female power and prowess. Men are peripheral, unnecessary, and boring.* This was long before the mass wave of my dyke friends becoming moms, so men weren't even useful as sperm donors yet. Was this a self-fulfilling prophecy?

As a butch dyke, I was a transgressive rebel. At least, that's what it felt like when I would exit a public women's restroom to find security guards waiting for me, because my presence frightened other patrons so much ("There is a *man* in the ladies' room!"). I could enter any public space and it would be like trumpets were sounding out that I was *queer*, that I was *a lover of women*, an *outlaw*. I spent many years living as a very masculine woman, a default identity location where I did my best to exist happily. The words that I used to describe myself swung with the weight of a splitting maul: *butch dyke*. The epiphany that I would be a happier human being if I could exist in the world as a man was terrifying.

GROWING UP in a Boston-area, Catholic, working-class-on-the-cusp-of-middle-class household, I was mired in the cultural belief that a terrible known is always much less frightening than the unknown of change, the unspoken corollary being that you don't deserve to be happy anyway. You are assigned a destiny that you must bear, a prearranged albatross cast in cement that you must carry forever. Change is hard because it requires choice.

Being queer created a delayed adolescence for many of my generation. We were on hold during developmental years, while we pretended to love boys or girls or football or proms, doing whatever it took to approximate *normal*. When we were ready and able to emerge and truly *be* ourselves, we often found ourselves left with a lot of growing up yet to do. Meanwhile, our non-queer peers were chipping away at being grown-ups under white supremacist, late-stage capitalism, with all of the signifiers of adulthood conveniently at their fingertips: careers, marriage, children, mortgages, material accumulation. For me, choosing to transition to male allowed me to finally become an adult. It was the first concrete decision I ever made in my life.

LIVING IN Santa Fe, I learned that transitioning in public is an awkward process. It now seems important that I had to live through the bizarre and sometimes hilarious experience of being thirty-three and suddenly going through puberty, only to accelerate back to staring down the hatch at near-middle-age in a matter of eight years. I often wished to run away, to banish myself to a mountainside Zen cave, but instead fielded questions about whether I had a persistent cold that kept my voice alternately froggy and squeaky for two years solid. I had to debate to whom and when to come out: *Do I come out to my jerk boss at my new job? To the woman at the coffee drive-through who has started to look at me quizzically when I roll up in my truck? Do I correct the waitress who calls me "she"? Is the Zia Diner at dinner rush an appropriate place for an ad-hoc Trans 101 workshop? Is it my imagination, or am I treated kindlier by the older Hispanic cashier lady at the grocery store, the more I am read as male?*

ONE NIGHT, when I'd been on testosterone for about six months, I was at the movies for another epic *Lord of the Rings* installment, and I had to use the restroom halfway through. At this point, I was read as male about fifty percent of the time. I walked toward the men's restroom, and out of my peripheral vision, saw that another guy was walking up close behind me—so at the very last second, I panicked and turned left into the women's room. The guy, on autopilot, followed me into the women's room, and locked himself in a stall. I don't think he ever noticed that both he and I were in the wrong restroom.

But now, after years of public restroom use being a site of conflict and fear, I was using men's restrooms and locker rooms without incident. I do need to report back, however, how infrequently men wash their hands after using a urinal.

I mentioned this to my girlfriend once, and she forbade me to ever speak of it again.

NON-TRANS people like the "born in the wrong body" idea because there is real comfort (for them) in binaries, of understanding that if you are not *A* then you must be *B*. A person must be one thing or the other, two categories, easily identifiable. The liminal space in-between two poles, which comprises a substantial part of a trans life, is very difficult to grasp. I really feel it now, as I move through the world in mostly blissful anonymity—read as "just a straight white man," the most boring kind of person on earth. A boringness that once scrutinized explodes into a kaleidoscope of historical privileges going back through eons. I feel like an "outsider within," a spy in the house of male. Sometimes, I'll go from spy to assassin—at least toward bad ideas that go unchallenged in spaces comprised solely of men.

I'VE ALWAYS related to the heartbreak of Roy Batty in the denouement of *Blade Runner,* when he says, "I've seen things you people wouldn't believe. Attack ships on fire off the shoulder of Orion. I watched C-beams glitter in the dark near the Tannhäuser Gate. All those moments will be lost in time . . . like tears in rain . . . " But the unbelievable things I've seen are largely composed of small wonders, fleeting joys, and fragments of human behavior filtered through the lens of being seen as entirely one gender and then another.

In the constellations of gender through which I've traversed, I've seen things that people who presume gender as fixed, innate, and unmoving would never conceive of as possible. I've watched the unbelievable adventure of transforming the only thing in this world I have control over: myself. And ultimately, I know that, while making permanent choices for an impermanent body, all of these moments will be lost in time.

MY SUMMER in Santa Fe ended up lasting eight years. While there, I had few models for transitioning and living as a trans man, and so I became a resource myself. When I gave something to others that I didn't have for myself, it somehow magically staved off a sense of scarcity for me—if you have something to give, then you have more than enough for yourself, right? I emerged from my time in the desert harder, sharper, tougher, and more precise. During my decision-making zenith, I decided to move to Portland, Oregon for graduate school and to pursue my writing full-time—somehow.

I was excited to rejoin the world along the I-5 corridor— life moves faster and more fluidly on the coasts—but also to live somewhere with a strong trans community and an abundance of resources. It occurred to me that this would be the first place I'd ever lived where my history would not be known by everyone around me, where I would just be seen as a man. *This will be a new chapter*, I thought. *No one will know my past or process unless I divulge it.* That idea filled me with relief and anxiety in equal measure.

The first time I went to my local dive bar in Portland, I was standing out front to smoke when two younger dykes walked up to me, fished their IDs out of their pockets, and presented them to me.

I laughed. "I don't work here, you guys!"

One of the girls shrugged, unmoved. "Well, you're a big guy with muttonchops and a Mötorhead T-shirt, standing out front. We thought you were carding."

"Ha, no. I just moved here like three days ago—"

But they were already fast on their way into the bar.

In Portland I learned how goddamn lonely it is to be a man. People don't talk much to men. Before class, I would walk to a local café, drink ridiculously good coffee, and write. I'm 5'9" and white, bearded, and heavily tattooed, so I blend in with 75 percent of Portland males. I'm not sure anyone would have ever struck up a conversation with me if not for my sweet old dog. He made me an approachable man. When I moved to San Francisco at twenty-three, I cruised into The Bearded Lady Café to find a room full of queers who welcomed me warmly. All I had to do was park myself at the café with my notebook to make friends, get invited to events, find a great room to rent in a shared household, or get laid. Community came by osmosis. Now here I was, almost twenty years later: alone, grown-up and male, invisible to my queer brethren, and ignorable to most.

When my graduate classes began, I made a point of swinging by the Queer Resource Center on campus. I wanted to find out what was going on at the university and how to get involved; how I might be of service. A few people were milling about, and I waited for someone to acknowledge me so that I could say hello. I was left to stare at the bulletin board announcing support groups and HIV testing sites. Soon, a gender-variant person on the more feminine end of the spectrum walked in and they were greeted with an exuberant "Hey, *girl!*" I was ignored.

A few days later, I returned with my lunch and asked if I could eat in the QRC lounge. The staff person said yes and gave me a quick tour of the center. People came and went, and I smiled and nodded, but I was convinced they were thinking, *What is this* dude *doing in here?* As I ate, I realized how hard it is to start over in a new place, especially when you're male, older, and pass as straight and probably cis. I wondered if maybe the thing making me the weirdest was, in fact, my age.

I finally connected with old friends who'd migrated here over the years, attended a monthly group for FTM guys, and experienced a glimpse of the bounty of Portland's legendary trans-friendliness. At my age, my community cannot, and should not, be built by osmosis, but through intention and care. I no longer worry that I will be a man caught between worlds, stuck in a liminal, *Ladyhawke*-like nonexistence, where my worlds connect in glimmering seconds between dark and light. But I do often feel the ache and thrum of Roy Batty's manmade manhood, how he was also a man without first being a boy, of seeing things that no one would ever believe, the twinning consciousness of straddling worlds, lives, genders.

For me, passing is a relief, a privilege, and at times, a curse. As a butch, my masculinity felt like a full-time job. My life and body were a billboard upon which I had to constantly paint my maleness. The more my body and physical appearance aligned with my self-perception mentally and emotionally, the less effort I put into being masculine, and the more energy I put into understanding what it means to be a masculine presence out in the world with care. I love being a man, now that I understand that to be a man is not just one thing. I'm grateful that I've been able to take claim of my life and shape it. It is no small thing to feel at home in your own skin, that others see you as you know yourself to be, that your body and brain finally run on the proper chemicals. I have traded life as a miserable and confused swashbuckling outlaw to become an adult. I have worked hard to be this boring.

Trans Grit

On the mild Sunday evening I became a trans curmudgeon, I sat circled up with two dozen others in folding chairs, all on a spectrum of gender in the neighborhood of my own. We ranged in age from high school to near retirement, many a year or less into transition, or else trying to decide whether or not to swing a leg over in this rodeo at all. I didn't seek support so much as a sense of connection, to be among others like me. Strange to progress from the constant of change to this *olde trans* status with no segue, no half-time show. All flux, and then it was everything else in life that I needed to deal with.

A YOUNG trans guy, anxious and lost in a mass of too-big clothes, shared with utter despondency that someone from a doctor's office was *rude* to him on the phone. He'd crumbled in the face of rudeness, his forward process stymied by the molasses of agonism, this ticket-taker saying, *you're too short to ride, sorry.* He'd hung up the phone, unable to access the care he needed.

Welcome to the rest of your life as a transsexual, I wanted to say, knowing well how *that* word—a word that hundreds of thousands of trans people had self-elected to use to describe themselves for over half a century—could be lobbed back at me with accusations of now being a slur, or at best, *unfashionable.* I slouched in my plastic chair like a delinquent student. A cascade of similar tales ricocheted around the room from other younger folks, volleyed in a manner that precluded any true listening or reflection.

You think rudeness *is the worst of it?* I thought. *Microaggressions? You cannot wither in the face of those who don't want to help you. You'll need to learn how to either charm them into being your greatest proponent or else clamp your will to their pant legs with the persistence of a pitbull until they help you.*

Voila. In an instant, I'd become that guy: *olde trans. A goddamn trans grouch.* Perhaps I no longer belonged at a meeting if I couldn't brim with empathy for the plight of this kid and his vexing phone call. Perhaps the agony, excitement, and wanting a high-five for each achievement was long gone for me. I joined this rodeo a decade and a half ago, and my ass was sore from years of rough riding. I was well-aware of the judgment that stewed in me and how little my Buddhist practice made a dip in that mucky soup. From across the room, I wanted to say, "Buck up, little camper. You're gonna have to be tougher than this. You're gonna need some grit to do this."

THE FOLDING plastic chair chewed at my back as I remembered the hurdles and trials and obstacles and violence and discrimination that trans people I know had to overcome for years to be who they are. We were busy confronting and surviving *macroaggressions* and lack of access. I thought of my early mentors, who smuggled, shared, and used black-market hormones, or friends who, long ago, lay alone in hotel rooms for a week post-surgery, with no one to help them—people I'd met who sought hormones and surgery from doctors twenty, thirty years ago, knapping a wheel out of stone. No Harry Benjamin to jump through, no WPATH to walk. People who turned tricks, went on fertility drugs and sold their eggs, or took out student loans to afford surgery—others who shot street steroids or self-castrated in prison. My trans women friends from the Navajo Nation, who told me stories about pumping parties on the rez, where women self-injected hardware-store silicone into their breasts. I thought about a friend whose almost *trans-mythological* tale about being forced to self-aspirate a hematoma in his chest after top surgery was known to me years before we'd ever met—and this was in pre-social networking days. I thought of the countless hours I'd spent being told, "No," that something was unavailable, illegal, or impossible. Or just not right, like a bearded man needing a pelvic ultrasound or mammogram. I thought of the time when, after many years of being on T and procuring top surgery without health insurance, I got coverage and made many long calls explaining to a middle-aged, white Texan man at the insurance company why the hysterectomy for which I was seeking pre-approval was not part of a not-covered "sex change."

"Look, Hal," I'd explained to this stranger, "I'm not trying to get away with anything here. These are just the parts I was born with, and they're causing me significant pain."

I was frustrated by these young trans people for being so easily discouraged and deterred. If transitioning taught me anything, it was that I needed to possess the will to do whatever it took to survive.

HE HELD a syringe loose in his hand, and with a flick of his hairy wrist, threw the point into the shiny, pocked skin of an orange, to its hilt. "Now you try, hold it like a dart." He pulled the needle free from the fruit and handed me both. My nervous fingers meant to crush the syringe, but I couldn't crush and dart at the same time. *Exhale.*

It took no effort to pierce the rind. I plunged a barrel full of air into the orange. Practice was over.

Back in the late '80s, he and his best friend carted black market hormones up from Mexico because there was no clinic back then for guys like us—a practice he has long since disavowed. He, who fucked with the lines in-between as creative praxis and sex art, was my trans lineage, my elder who hewed a clearing for people like me. I lay facedown on the bed with my belt and dirty jeans snugged down to the peak of my ass. He directed my girlfriend to push the dart into the meat at the center of a Bermuda triangle found with my hands. My first shot of T, and I chickened out of giving it to myself.

The warm oil was a small punch under my skin that might bruise later. "You can do what you want, but I suggest going full-dose at first so you know what it feels like," he said. And that was the entire point of this whole experiment: for me to know what it felt like to be on Vitamin T. For so long I wondered, trying to convince myself I didn't need to. Never being able to really let it go. The anxiety and discomfort and disconnect growing deeper and wider, a canyon cut through the years of a sandstone life, not ever quite fully alive. Now, I would have empirical evidence, a way to compare and contrast. A way to make an informed decision, once and for all, I hoped. My friend was my teacher, because seventeen years ago, that's what we had. Just each other.

THE MODERN history of us is so short that we must consciously choose to forget, to unknow, or to never learn in the first place. We are rankled and dogged by the obstacles of systems, protocols, bureaucracies. We peevishly acquiesce to the binary simplicity of the State because it is easier to leave more than breadcrumbs along our paper trails, or else we don't or can't, and any minor errand becomes a hassle in having to prove you are real. "I exist, I am possible," we say, standing right in front of their incredulous/condescending/confused/irritated faces. A piece of embossed paper seems more real than me in front of you. Standards of care can be problematic, a short leash pulling against our necks. Held up against history, old negatives to the yellow light of a window: before then, we got imprisoned, lobotomized, electroshocked, institutionalized. Before and before and before, we existed and we guarded the secret of our existences until our deaths, before that we were burned or drowned, and maybe long before all of that we were revered.

Let's always believe that, hold on to that—that maybe we were once respected, like astronauts or creatures that climbed from the froth of the sea to live on land, held in wonder because of the worlds we've straddled, and for all of the wisdom we've gathered there, in both and in between places.

AFTER SO many years, I worked up the nerve to cruise into the Tom Waddell Clinic in San Francisco's Tenderloin for what we then, with great affection, referred to as "Tranny Tuesdays." The trans clinic had originally opened in the early '90s to serve a swath of trans women and transfeminine people who were being pummeled by AIDS. It was a place that practiced a harm reduction ethos and prioritized trans people who were sex workers, IV drug users, or surviving on the streets. Even in 2002, it was the only place I knew to go.

I waited in a dim hallway in a bucket chair and told the narrative I believed that I had to in order to convince anyone I was "trans enough" to be on hormones. I would've liked to say that I wanted to know what it was like to be on T so that I could make an informed decision based on experience. It was my first day of many years of saying whatever I had to, sketching out binary tropes and half-truths, to get what I needed from some authority figure, and saving my activism for outside of the examination room. I couldn't fight both battles in the same moment.

"The lower exam is important," my doctor tried to reassure me. "I'll be swift."

"Don't worry about it. I'll just leave my body anyway," I said. She didn't find this funny, but humor was as vital a survival tool as dissociation was.

I sank against the examination table in my flimsy gown. She came back into the room with Raquel, the physician's assistant. Raquel was desert-weathered and handsome, a middle-aged Latina from a small Mormon town in Colorado, where half the populace was her family. Her people had lived there for two centuries. Raquel flirted while cinching the boa constrictor of the blood pressure cuff around my bicep. She always knew how to strum that chord of making a person feel good and appreciated without hitting the note of implied expectation, the light of a match struck but no fire set.

"How have you been, *novio*?" Raquel pumped the bulb and smiled. "You haven't come by to see me lately. Staying out of trouble?"

We were from different worlds, but we found commonalities, like growing up with neighbors who happened to be multiple generations of your family.

I'd never known if Raquel knew I was trans; now, with my bare feet in the cold stirrups and my knees apart, there wasn't much she wouldn't know. My guts gurgled like a clogged toilet; my cheeks flamed. I stared myself away at the composite ceiling tiles until the cold jelly fingers and pain was over. It only lasted two minutes, but time pulled long and thin.

After, Raquel came back in with some paperwork. I'd assumed, with no context for someone like me, that her behavior toward me would change. But she still flirted in her warm way—that day, and as long as she worked there.

A year later, she would assist my doctor in aspirating a hematoma, a purple aquifer blooming in my freshly-sutured-flat chest. The universe knocked me over the head with the cosmic skillet of this lesson: People are so much more willing to understand us than we ever give them credit for. And we spend so much time and energy convincing non-trans people of the truth that we are a vulnerable and victimized population that sometimes we forget how fucking strong and resilient we are. These things can exist in tandem: recognizing the injustices against us and celebrating the fortitude it takes for each of us to live in this world.

I MADE an appointment with the county clinic for a round of regular STI testing. *Oh, Portland, you trans nirvana*, I thought, checking off boxes on the intake form, which was peppered with a multiverse of sex, gender, sexual orientation, et cetera, et cetera. Male: *check!* Transgender: *check!* Queer: *check!* A clinician went through my intake form, asking why I was there and about my various sexual practices. With the tip of her pen, she poked a stamp-sized line drawing of a cock and balls at the bottom of the form. "Anything unusual going on for you here? Swelling, itching, sores . . . ?"

"Just so you know, I'm trans."

A silent *Oh!* widened the aperture of her mouth. "So . . . what you're saying is…this picture doesn't really apply to you."

"Exactly."

She tapped my upper arm, trying to recover the blunder. "Well, good job! I never would've guessed."

"Well, I *did* check all of the boxes," I said, trying to figure out a non-violent way of informing her that anointing me with a "good job" implied that there are trans people who are *not* doing a good job, and that this is highly problematic, because being trans isn't a fucking contest. The clinician was kind and dedicated to community health, and I knew she was *doing*—was *trying*—her best.

This was what the best looked like in trans nirvana, and I was okay with it because at least I didn't feel thwarted, judged, or scared. Patience and willingness to be honest and uncomfortable, to make and transcend mistakes is an arrow that extends in two directions.

The next time I went to the county health office for routine STI testing, I was elated and relieved to discover that my clinician was a trans woman. It was my first time in a medical office where I felt like I could speak all of my truth. I didn't need to shuffle my history and pick out the cards I felt I needed to show in order to get the treatment I needed. I could fan out the whole deck.

MY ASS was half-asleep. I hadn't been listening to the meeting at all. My consciousness floated back into the room. It was easier to be frustrated than to look within, because at the bottom of my curmudgeonly feelings was a *worry for the very survival of any trans person*. In these memories, just a fraction of many, I held the aggregate of these frictions, this compiled weight.

It *is* exhausting. I think this kid, whom I was so quick to judge, maybe had it right all along: We *should* feel annoyed and outraged when we aren't met with helpful service in a medical system for which we pay so much in time, energy, and money—and in lives. His distress and frustration at this poor treatment is probably a good thing: It means we, as a demographic, have evolved enough to believe *we deserve better*. A momentum that started decades before I transitioned is still in a hard swing, the force of which means that now, trans people expect a fuck of a lot better. While many things have improved for us, we still have so much further to go. This road was easier for me because of the suffering, struggle, activism, and work of those who came before me.

One day, seventeen years from now, this kid might scoff and roll his eyes, hearing about how easy a kid who transitions has it. Maybe in 2037, we won't even call it transitioning anymore. My trans curmudgeon status might be here to stay, but I realize the kid's expectation for kind helpfulness is a result of trans suffering in the halls of institutionalized medicine, and that his outrage can, and will, become part of a collective lever that ratchets our broken system to a new and better place.

Holding on with Both Hands

In the beginner's mind there are many possibilities,
but in the expert's there are few.
—SHUNRYU SUZUKI

I banged out five pull-ups on the bar I'd just installed in the doorjamb of my kitchen.

"Must be nice to be on testosterone," my butch house-mate, Jan, drawled from the couch. It wasn't her first subtle jab about the gulf between our identities that some days felt wider than others.

My cheeks flushed with irritation. T did not anoint me, or anyone, with special abilities—though it wasn't the first time someone had made a comment suggesting this was the case. I wanted to volley back that when I first decided I wanted to be able to do pull-ups, my then-girlfriend could whip out countless reps. She was the one who coached me from zero to hero—and *she* wasn't on T. I wanted to point out all of Jan's other trans guy friends, many of whom couldn't do pull-ups or chin-ups, never mind the male-born-men we all knew, who couldn't eke out a single chin-up. I thought about all the musclehead dudes and gym rats at my gym, who avoided the pull-up bar with a wide berth. I wanted to swat back: *Maybe if you want to do pull-ups, you could take better care of yourself, stop self-medicating with weed and beer. Just put your time into something you really* want.

I was sick of people weighing in on my life, minimizing or judging or scrutinizing. Something that I'd learned in my new life as an adult male, which had only started ten years prior—was that everything that came out of my mouth while looking like this was weighted differently. What I said while taking up space in the world as a man *meant* differently. So I bit my tongue.

IT WAS a hard, humiliating place to be, hanging red-faced, aching, and panting from the pull-up bar at the local community center gym. My core muscles felt like they were about to rip apart, and my fingers screamed with effort. I'd hurtle myself up to the bar however I could, hands burning from the sticky, blackened athletic tape wound around the bar, and lower myself as slowly as I could. Negative repetitions. It was not comfortable. Not being any good at something is uncomfortable. Trying to do it anyway is uncomfortable.

When I'd be about to reach the bottom extension, my then-girlfriend or our workout buddy Drey would place a palm between my shoulder blades and shove me back up to the bar. At first, just two or three reps of this were enough to cause full-body pain. My hands would be red and raw, stuck in a half-curl. But eventually, I could slow my descending body, stretching each rep to thirty seconds or more.

Callouses replaced the raw, red spots on my palms. Finally, after weeks of this, I hauled myself up to the bar, chin clearing the top. I did it—I did a pull-up. High-fives all around.

I thought back to the humiliation of the Presidential Fitness Test in middle school—those commercials with Arnold in his robo-fascist accent, the standing broad jumps, sit-ups, and for girls, hanging from the chin-up bar. They didn't even expect girls to try, nor did our gym teachers want to help you work it out. Now, I was in my mid-to-late thirties, and this was the first pull-up of my life.

Why did Jan's comment chap my caboose so hard? It had little to do with the pull-ups, I realized. Pull-ups were just a metaphor. Jan saw testosterone as a magic wand waved over my life, something that gave me special powers and strength. It seemed she saw testosterone as the lucky rabbit's foot that fixed my life, since she was never going to transition, she let all of us know, loudly, though I'd never asked. Maybe that was her *out,* and now she didn't have to fix her own life. *If only* my life was "fixed" by transitioning, my problems vanquished, my self-work done.

It was only after choosing to transition that I wanted anything from this life, that I was able to choose anything. Before that, I was adrift, a ghost ship floating on a dark sea. In choosing to transition, I was choosing to live, and choosing to be the captain of my ship, to inhabit my life. A few years back I'd made a powerful discovery: *I am the only person responsible for my life.* Despite where I came from, how I grew up, what I'd been through, my fuck-ups, what had happened to me—what happened next was *my* responsibility. Having a list of goals was new to me, having lived for so long in a state of survival, where all my energy went to meeting my day-to-day needs. Being able to do pull-ups was just one tiny task on the list of things I wanted to accomplish, now that my life had actually begun. My new list ranged from learning pull-ups and benching 225, to doing some major healing work, to learning how to be an adult in my intimate relationships, to getting an MFA and making writing and art my (full-time) career, to getting my books published.

My irritation fizzled as quickly as it had flared, replaced by a pang of compassion. I saw myself in Jan. I'd *been* her. I, too, had spent years in a stasis-like slow suicide. I'd sat on the couch feeling angry at other people for doing their own thing, instead of focusing on what I steps I could take toward what I want. Being in a masculine female body meant that she walked through the world as a backstop onto which people projected their unexamined bullshit, something I knew firsthand. It wasn't for me to tell her any of this, either, just to be a silent witness. Jan would find her own way on her own timeline. I *wanted* her to be happy.

"No," I said instead, wiping my palms on my jeans. "I can do pull-ups because I've worked hard at pull-ups."

Man Pageant, Unscripted

In Portland, Oregon's historic Crystal Ballroom, the house lights dim, ambient music fades, and the roar of voices coalesce into a delighted hum of anticipation. Beer sloshes from plastic cups onto shirts and shoes as the crowd surges forward, and the warm footlights glow onto hirsute men strutting across the stage, flaunting follicles that are Melvillian to near-monstrous in size and style. Their aesthetics range from gutter punk to American Gothic. They are young and old, slim and stocky, foreign and local, from every vocation, class, ethnicity, and sexual identity. What these men all share is facial hair worthy of competition.

The first annual West Coast Beard and Mustache Championships is people-watching at its prime. Many patrons sport sculpted facial fur. Some also swagger in fanciful outfits that complement their bearded bounty. The multigenerational crowd abounds with bowler derby hats, ascots, and canes, along with lederhosen and German barmaid dresses, leather pants, tattoos, peacoats and Greek fisherman caps, and top hats. Cephalopod-like mustaches seem to wriggle forth on their owners' faces, curling tentacles of hair defying gravity. There is at least one Abraham Lincoln. A man in his late thirties is dressed like a garden gnome, with a red, very tall, conical hat and a flowing blue blouse. His long, reddish beard comes to a gnomish point somewhere around his xiphoid process. One young man rocks a WWII-era officer's dress uniform, while his companion wears a full Scotsman's outfit, complete with a peaked cap and kilt, complemented by his full, rusty-brown mustache and Van Dyke. Their chins raise and their chests balloon when I ask if I can take their picture.

While my own facial crop is far from contest-worthy, I jump at the chance to attend such a bountiful celebration of the man-flag. As a transgender man, the ability to finally grow facial hair was an enormous milestone in my journey to *male*. It took years of hormone therapy, but now I can grow a beard or mustache that exceeds that of a teenager. I go to learn—like many trans people, I'm a perpetual student of gender—to see what I might divine about maleness and masculinity. I go as a spy, undetectable as anyone other than a man who's always had the promise of facial hair on his horizon.

I grasp my own plastic cup of bland beer and make my way toward the stage through the throng of attendees. I attend by myself, and unburdened by idle chitchat or the impatience of others, I'm free to explore. I'm on my own private anthropological investigation.

The judges take their seats at a table festooned with a hand-painted banner for the Stumptown Stash and Beard Collective, whose logo depicts a beaver wearing a handlebar mustache and standing atop a stump. The judge wearing a white polo shirt and ball cap is Phil Olsen, president of Beard Team USA. He strokes his stately beard with a soft brush as he contemplates the line-up. It is time for round one: Natural Mustache.

Phil Olsen started in Bearding while traveling in Ystad, Sweden in 1999. It was a coincidence that he happened upon the World Beard and Mustache Championships, hosted by the *Svenska Mustaschklubben*—the Swedish Mustache Club.

"I had a substantial beard at the time and fit in really well," says Phil, whose dark, rounded beard and gruff demeanor belie a surprisingly musical voice, like a radio announcer or voice-over actor. Phil is the founder, acting president, and frequent competition judge of Beard Team USA, as well as the visionary who introduced the sport of Bearding to the United States. "I take full credit for the trend," says Phil. "The people who know me recognize what I've done for the sport. People close to me know how hard I've worked."

"America was underrepresented," he says of the 1999 Worlds, Phil's shorthand for the international championships. "Most of the competitors were Germans. I speak German and they thought it was pretty cool." In 2001, the

Association of German Beard Clubs asked Phil to organize in the United States. He started Beard Team USA in 2003 at the Worlds in Carson City, California.

"Bearding is the easiest sport there is," Phil Olsen says. "To get started, you do nothing." Still, the recent surge of interest in facial hair is difficult to explain. "[Bearding] is a natural thing." Phil pauses. "Being clean-shaven is unnatural. Shaving is altering your appearance, removing a masculine characteristic. Shaving is for men who want to look like women."

This doesn't necessarily describe men who, due to genetics or heredity, can't grow much of a beard, but Phil sees that as just *their* natural state. "They can save it or shave it. I would admire those who save it, but I would understand those who shave it, thinking it doesn't look good." For those whose profession requires them to be clean-shaven, he says, "I feel sorry for those guys. The requirements are irrational, but that is the fault of those adopting the requirements, not those who must comply with them." Pity a man who suffers from pogonophobia—an extreme dislike or fear of beards.

It's not that a lack of facial hair makes a man less of a man; rather, Phil advocates for men to celebrate this aspect of masculinity if they so choose. "Men who want to have beards should have beards. Men who want to look like women should look like women. I believe most men want to have beards. Too many of them shave because they think someone else wants them to." Despite his provocative, pro-beard quips, Phil's stance on gender is not so black-and-white. He doesn't think that women who can grow a natural beard are trying to look like men, he thinks they are trying to look more like themselves. "Since such women are a very small minority of women, it takes a lot of courage to let their beards grow. I would not criticize them for shaving it in order to avoid being a curiosity." Phil is adamant that everyone feel welcome in the sport, whatever their facial hair ability or proclivity.

I asked Phil what inspired him to grow a beard. "I didn't 'grow' a beard, it just grew," he says. "I am not sure—is it evolution or creation?"

A semi-retired lawyer, Phil says that having a large, full beard hasn't affected his work. In fact, he gets exclusively positive comments on it. "I am very fastidious in maintaining it—it adds to my professionalism."

Part of the mission of Beard Team USA is advocacy. He says that some believe having heavy facial hair is akin to uncleanliness, like not showering or brushing your teeth. "I am breaking prejudice by showing that a beard can complement a person's appearance." The mission statement on his website declares that "BTUSA opposes discrimination against the bearded, mustached, sideburned, and goateed." Phil has, on several occasions, written letters to various organizations requesting that they permit an employee to have a beard.

Some employers have a strict dress code which precludes beards; others try to enforce a "look policy." For many employees whose workplaces fall under the at-will employment doctrine, there is little protection from being fired if having facial hair violates the dress code, unless firing the employee can be demonstrated to violate religious freedoms, anti-discrimination laws, or medical exceptions.

"We oppose discrimination in any form and are open to fighting it. But the more effective strategy is to set an example. Beards are [becoming] more accepted. I don't feel out of place in a courtroom because I have a beard."

TO DATE, there have been three beard competitions in Portland. The first one was in September 2010, an outdoor event at the Portland Pirate Festival, an annual event that features historical reenactments, music, dance, and interactive theater. Phil Olsen was a judge at that one, too. "It poured rain most of the time, but nobody seemed to notice but me," says the Tahoe City resident. He sees Portland as a great city for beards, but is quick to add, "You could talk to lots of people and they would say *their* city is a great place for beards. Beards are growing everywhere."

Phil is not sure which chapter of Beard Team USA is the largest. The Stumptown Stash and Beard Collective is very active, as is the Charleston, South Carolina group, which is hosting a competition soon. The Los Angeles chapter also sponsors a competition.

"I made an effort for [Beard Team USA] to not be like the Rotary Club. There are no rules, no dues, no secret handshake." Phil says the goal is "to have fun and spread Bearding."

The Beard Team USA website states that:

> *Membership in America's team is open to everyone. There are no annoying applications, dues, membership requirements, or gender tests. Unlike some sporting organizations, Beard Team USA encourages the use of performance-enhancing substances.*

Phil sees the family-friendly atmosphere as part of the inclusive nature of the sport. "In Portland, there were lots of families; people brought their kids. Everyone has a great time. It's universal—the camaraderie is what the events are for, everyone agrees. People from different walks of life find friendship through an odd interest. In Sweden, I saw that it brings people together. I encourage people of different ages, locations, countries, religions, languages, racial backgrounds to get involved—I want everyone to feel included. The competition should be playful. It's all in fun, but it's not a joke."

DURING THE third round of the WCBMC, Full Natural Beard with Styled Mustache, a woman standing beside me in the audience declares, "It's like a *man* pageant." The WCBMC contestants are not unlike male birds strutting their splendid plumage. There are few opportunities that I can think of for men to be admired for their looks in this way. I wonder what a contest like this says about cisgender men's desire to feel...*beautiful*, if such pageantry is an important outlet missing from our culture. What exactly is the cultural significance of a facial hair competition?

"It's about men wanting to look like men," Phil says.

AT AGE seven, I'd lather Barbasol on my face, thick as cake frosting. It was easy to imagine my beard beneath the white, shaving-cream shadow on my reflected visage. I'd slap my cheeks loudly with my father's aftershave, breathing in the wonderful stink of musky lime—*Hai Karate!* The alcohol was cool, then dried with a sting. My father had shaved off his beard before leaving for his two-week summer Army drills, and I freaked. *Who was that man standing at my father's sink?* I always knew I'd grow up to have facial hair—somehow.

THE INDEPENDENT Film Channel (IFC) recently premiered its latest reality show, *Whisker Wars,* bringing national attention to the subculture of Bearding. The program was created by producer Thom Beers, who has graced cable television with other testosterone-pumped hits like *Deadliest Catch*, *Ice Road Truckers*, *Ax Men*, and *Coal*.

According to Phil Olsen, *Whisker Wars* "has raised the profile of the sport and created tremendous interest." He says that he's been working toward that level of exposure for competitive Bearding for years, but he now sees negativity and hostility, where previously there was none. "The show thrives on conflict—that was never a part of Bearding before. We never had booing or disrespect." It is no surprise to Phil that programs like this trump up disaccord. "It is unnecessary to create drama. As long as you are inquisitive and perceptive, you can see the drama that is already there; you don't need to inject it. I try to promote the integrity of the sport and to welcome everyone, to make it friendly and open. I've tried to make it as transparent and fair as possible."

Phil says that the big competitions are a fairly new thing. They've been catching on since 2009, and now there seems to be an event almost every couple of weeks. Phil sounds as serious as a heart attack when it comes to fairness and appropriateness in his sport. It's *not* a joke, after all. But drama is the meat of reality television. As Thom Beers told *The Hollywood Reporter*: ". . . it's [about] finding a culture where there are rules and codes, heroes and villains. That's what's fascinating to me."

"The most important thing is to have a fair contest and avoid the appearance of impropriety," Phil says, reminding me of something Norman Mailer wrote: "Masculinity is not something given to you, but something you gain. And you gain it by winning small battles with honor."

JUSTIN CATE, founder of both the Stumptown Stash and Beard Collective, the WCBMC, and the emcee of tonight's event, thinks of Bearding as just another arena for men to be competitive. "I don't think it says anything necessarily about manhood, but it does illustrate the ability of social networking to be able to foster the growth of a group, consisting of just about any demographic one can imagine. Before this modern competitive scene started, facial hair may have been a way to display individuality, and show indifference to the standard, corporate way of life. Now, though, it seems to have become chic, or another fad that has infiltrated society."

Phil developed his signature beard technique over the years. Like asking a famous chef to divulge their secret ingredient, it seems rude to ask how he achieves this magical roundness. "It appeals to me, so I keep it that way," he says, but he freely offers general Bearding wisdom: "You have to start experimenting with different ways to style, shape, condition, and groom your beard. It has to fit your personality. My main advice is to have fun with it."

THERE ARE many women in the audience at the WCBMC, and quite a few are strolling the ballroom in mustaches. Some are Fu Manchu-types cut from black felt, others are more convincing—thick, synthetic hair, attached with spirit gum. As far as I can tell, there are no naturally mustachioed or bearded women present. At least two women compete in the Freestyle Mustache heat, albeit with artificial mustaches. The crowd whoops and hollers right along for them, especially for the woman in a German Fräulein dirndl, which accentuates both her cleavage and the humongous handlebar mustache that extends several inches beyond each cheek into the festive air. She roars like a lioness while two-fisting steins of beer above her head. The crowd goes bananas.

Phil wants everyone to feel included and to have fun in Bearding, and says the women are welcomed by the guys. "Any woman with a real beard should enter the competition." The fake beard category has been historically conflated with the ladies' category, but he doesn't agree with that practice. "There shouldn't be categories between men and women, it should be just divided by real beards and fake beards." After a pause, Phil adds, "I feel sorry for women who have to put on a fake beard to have a beard."

I RECENTLY shaved clean for the first time since last August for a job interview, even though nobody asked me to. I didn't have the hugest beard—there are fourteen-year-old boys and grandmothers who can grow a more robust beard than I can—but it was over six months of intensive growing, and I was quite fond of my biggest, longest beard to date. There was something comforting about it, like a security blanket or a favorite hat. It was also like keeping a pet like a small rodent or lizard—a living thing that required at least a minimum of human interaction every day. It'll be a long time, if ever, before I'll be able to compete in the Full Natural Beard category.

However, I experienced a bit of chin dysphoria when I shaved. I couldn't believe how tiny and pale my chin seemed. In fact, it took me a couple of weeks to accept that this was now my face: my beardless, gray, shorn face. I just didn't feel quite like myself for a while. I asked Justin Cate if this is normal.

"I shaved just after I realized that I wouldn't be able to go to the 2009 Worlds," he said. "That was one of the only times I've seen my chin in the last fifteen years or so…the last time I shaved, I felt a little naked. I don't know that I'll shave anytime soon, as my beard has become a part of my personality."

THE CRYSTAL BALLROOM crowd is getting drunker, the cheering rowdier. During the fourth heat, Full Natural Beard, a stranger wearing dark glasses, a black fedora, and a huge, black mustache nudges my elbow and points at a contestant's antics. We laugh together. I've been having a ball all night, and the source of my ache-inducing smiling is the joy of diversity. It's the pleasure of witnessing flaunted difference—the amazingness in how alike, and yet unalike, we all are.

My Life in Ink

When I was eleven years old, I drew tattoos in thick pencil on this shiny-surfaced paper recycled from my father's work and sold the little hearts and anchors to kids at school for a nickel. I was a shitty capitalist even then, and a real softy when a kid wanted one of my tattoos but didn't have the cash. To apply my tattoos, all a kid had to do was lick their skin, stick the tiny drawing graphite-side down, and press for a count of three. I didn't make much money, but soon half the children in my grade were running through the school hallways with smudgy ships, dragons, and unicorns blackening their skinny forearms.

My first tattoo was (and still is) a crappy ankh on my right pinky finger. I did it myself with a safety pin and ink from one of my rapidograph pens. It was 1987, and I was in art school and blossoming into an aqua-netted, deathy, punk-rock wonder. I was all about the Egyptian Book of the Dead and found joy in anything angry or morbid. Really, I was desperate to find a way to live inside my own skin—to hang curtains and call it home and thereby find a way to exist in this world. Covering myself with tattoos seemed like a good start.

I was the first of my various circles of friends to get tattooed. In 1987, I was a veritable dolphin through the reef. During my first year at MassArt, an older and spectacularly goth girl named Patti Day told me she was getting tattooed. *Where? With who?* I desperately wanted to know. *I want tattoos!* Patti invited me to her apartment in Allston, and soon after my arrival, a dapper, biker-looking guy knocked on the door. He carried two small suitcases, and made small talk in a calm, quiet voice. His name was Mark.

Mark unpacked his equipment with nimble swiftness, and soon he was stepping on his pedal, revving his tattoo gun like a race car at a stoplight. He examined the needle bar as it flicked in and out of the tip of the filler tube like a hummingbird's tongue. He wore drugstore reading glasses far down on his nose like a grandmother, which only managed to make him look even cooler and tougher. He sat up and glanced from me to Patti.

"Okay. Who's first?" No turning back now.

Tattooing was illegal in Massachusetts then, an enforcement that lasted from the late 1960s until the turn of the century. Boston's ports brimmed with sailors wanting ink, but when a wave of hepatitis passed through the city's tattoo parlors, the state chose to shut down rather than regulate. In the year 2000, Massholes from P-town to Worcester could celebrate the *fin de siècle* with tattoos from their hometowns rather than traveling to New York, New Hampshire or, as I did, the underground.

Mark gave me two tattoos in Patti's flat that evening. I also got his business card, and shortly after, started scheduling him for tattoo parties at my Mission Hill apartment. My friends would come up to Boston from the South Shore on the Red Line, and Mark would arrive looking handsome and biker-tough with his little cases, and tattoo six or eight of us in an evening. I got to know my underground tattoo artist well enough to have actual conversations with him and hear him laugh. We were kids, getting silly things etched onto us forever, as if there would never be a tomorrow—a tomorrow where you might want to cover up that Eye of Horus. If he thought we were goofy, he was gracious enough to never let on. He carried a solemn manner of decorum and he would only accept a cold beer from us after the last person was bandaged up—very professional.

Years later, I discovered photos of Mark in Nan Goldin's book, *The Ballad of Sexual Dependency*, from 1978—a decade before I started getting tattoos from him. In the Nan Goldin pictures, he looks skinny, shining with sweat and drugs, young and big-eyed, a bloody, bandaged tattoo on his thin hip. I remember wishing I still had a way of contacting him. I had so many questions about him and all of the people in that book. *What it was like to be looked at by Nan through her camera? What it was like to look back and see yourself in the* book, *fixed in a time you most likely outgrew—that is, if you survived it? What it was like for Nan to look back through her corpus of work and see all of those friends who were now dead?*

In 1990, I had a girlfriend who was a tattoo artist—and not a great one. Maybe just an okay one. She learned how on the carnival circuit. She tried to teach me how to tattoo, but she didn't have the patience for me and my Taurus ways. (I also don't think she knew enough herself to impart instruction to anyone else). She once tore the gun out of my hands while I was working on her leg; impatient and hot-headed, she finished it herself, grumbling like I was an idiot.

When I moved to San Francisco in 1993, there was an abundance of great artists from whom to get tattooed. I promptly got a sacred heart in memory of my brother from the legendary Freddie Corbin. I then began to frequent Ed Hardy's shop in North Beach, long before his name started blowing up on soap bottles and lighters at Walgreens and on the T-shirts of suburban dads.

In those early days of my SF tenure, I lived in a renowned queer house in the Lower Haight, 122 Webster, home of the Webster Street Witches. One day, I answered a knock at my door. I figured it was one of the local crack aficionados wanting to borrow matches, but to my surprise, there were two ethereal girls swaying on my stoop and holding hands.

"We heard you did tattoos will you give us tattoos?" they asked with nary a comma, like *Children of the Corn* or something.

I eyeballed them hard. One was short and dark-haired, with a croaking amphibian voice and a huge septum piercing glimmering above a wispy mustache and slight beard. All of her clothes were the same color brown as her eyes, hair, and beard. The other girl was tall and ghostly in bleached hair and a cream-colored Victorian gown that was street-sooty and tattered at the hem. They wore a vegan pallor that made them seem like a sepia-tone tintype come to life. They still swayed back and forth slightly, as if to a breeze or unheard music, but my guess was heroin.

"I'm not a tattoo artist, you guys. Sorry."

They just stared at me harder in their close, narcotic way. "Will you give us tattoos anyway?"

"No. I'm sorry." Which felt difficult to say during a time of my life where I seemed to be saying YES to everything else.

But not long after, 1994 or something, there I was in the same house, drinking cold beers with Shanna Banana, giving each other jailhouse tattoos with sewing needles bundled tight with cotton thread and Waterman India ink blobbed into an upturned beer bottlecap. We watched *The Decline of Western Civilization* on VHS and gave each other tattoos that read "Sister" to the sounds of the Germs and X, as if we could etch the punk times we missed out on for being too young into each other's shoulders. Like Exene sang, *we were desperate*. Our friends were dying of AIDS, suicide, overdoses, so we tried to give each other something that would last.

Just a couple of years later, I landed an actual tattoo

apprenticeship at Black and Blue, next door to Red Dora's Bearded Lady. This was an amazing and generous opportunity that I completely squandered—not out of laziness, but maybe from immaturity, and definitely from doing too much. I swirled in some kind of energetic, fugue state of grief, terrified of ever spending two minutes alone with myself. So, when I took the apprenticeship, I was in a band called Dirt Bike Gang—as lead singer, I wrote most of our lyrics; I created huge oil paintings and a series of laborious, hand-drawn punk band posters; I landed several art shows; and I wrote furiously and performed often. I was at a creative zenith. I also worked three jobs; slept with just about *everyone*; attempted to drown my grief in booze, drugs, and cigarettes; and was housing my dear friend Atom in my bedroom for several months. In the spirit of saying YES to everything, I took on the tattoo apprenticeship on top of everything else I could barely juggle, a serious endeavor that requires commitment, responsibility, and focus—things I couldn't seem to access in my life until just a few years ago. So, for a few months, I soldered lots of tattoo needles onto holder bars, made signs for the shop, and flirted with all of the girls who came into a dyke-owned tattoo shop to be inked up and flirted with proper. Then, in the summer of 1997, I left to go on tour with Sister Spit.

I'm not sure who wanted me to do it first or how the tattooing even started. I tattooed about half our crew with jailhouse-style (the parlance these days is "stick and poke"), commemorative tour tattoos—scraggly stars with uneven arms, like baby starfish, or a star with the initials O and K on either side to salute our beloved OK Van (RIP). One had a little trail of stardust like a shooting star; it may have been to camouflage a mistake, but a couple of them came out . . . not half-bad! I gave them in bars, on a picnic table at a Texas anarchist compound, and in a living room in Buffalo. I wanted mine on my hand, but I couldn't bear to do a lumpy star on my own hand, so triple-Virgo and future Sister Spit tour member Stanya gave me a lovely little star on the web of my right hand in Williamsburg. I accept that in this instance, I could not take what I was willing to dish out. That's okay. It's *true*.

I could not and would not vouch for the quality of my work. I would agree to do it if the person agreed that they were okay with being possibly quite bummed about the result. It was a bit of a surprise that others wanted their tour tattoos after seeing the first or second. They were shaky and uneven but weirdly full of heart. I don't know anyone, myself included, who gets homemade tattoos with sewing needles and India ink because they want an excellent tattoo. It's about having the power and autonomy to make something that will stay around as long as our finite bodies will. It's about an immediacy, an intimacy, an indelible souvenir of a time and of a place that you will never return to as you sail forth in your life's own ocean. It is about a connection, a reminder, a friendship, an adventure. You can look at your scraggly little star and remember: *I was there.*

The Love That Remains

I always used to dream of the past
But like they say yesterday never comes
Sometimes there's a song in my brain
And I feel that my heart knows the refrain
I guess it's just the music that brings on nostalgia
For an age yet to come"
—BUZZCOCKS, "NOSTALGIA"

I listen to my friend Brook talk about her obsession with the dyke culture of 1990s San Francisco, a scene I was part of and she was not. She wonders aloud if there is a word that describes a sense of nostalgia for a time in which you did not live. I say that I imagine this hypothetical word would have to be German, with no direct English equivalent.

I long to let her soak in the warm pool of memories that flood my hippocampus. That time was my queer coming-of-age, comparable perhaps to high school or college days for more well-adjusted, normative folks. I smile and paste the layers of time together, imagine Brook delirious and sweaty on the dancefloor at Muff Dive, making out with other dykes in the dank, graffiti-brindled men's room, where the girls backed their asses up to the urinal to piss. *In our messy packs, weren't there always trans women back then, bellied up to the bar, hooking elbows with us in the pit at shows as we skanked in the chaos?* Gender was a wet paper bag we were all busy punching our way out of, so we could choose what we jumped back into.

In this *MAD* fold-in of my chronology, the past and present press toward each other to make a seamless picture. But on some days, the misty, glowing corona of memory fades and in the harsh light of last call, I can't see the me nor Brook of now, neither of us, in that picture.

I FIND one German word. It's close, but not quite right: *sehnsucht (['ze:nzʊxt] or zeen-zhot)*, a German noun that denotes an intense longing or pining, a deep emotional state. Sometimes it's used to describe life's longings. Perhaps it encompasses something of our unfinished business, the repairs we never managed to make, the canvases leaning unfinished against a cinderblock wall.

MY FRIEND Brook is a lesbian trans woman. She is ten years younger than me, and even younger in "trans years." I love hanging out with her because she's smart and funny and alive; she's a smokejumper who can parachute into the fire of any social situation, and she will meet it with the sheer power of her extroversion. She's game for just about anything. Despite the shitty stuff she's experienced in life, her compass always swivels to a magnetic north of positivity, and we are alike in that way. We both relish the feast of *tonight* like survivors, like we might be dead tomorrow. Because we both know that we might be. We both know that life is fleeting and ephemeral and filled with impossible brutality and loss, but also the most gorgeous messy joys and phosphorescent blazes of connection, so why not gather as many of those fragile branches of light to your breast as you can and try to build a nest? How can we make it so that you can see the body of all your myths in the sky?

> *"To look forward to the history that will be, one must look at and retell the history that has been told."*
> —JONATHAN GOLDBERG, "THE HISTORY THAT WILL BE"

Brook has a stamina and enthusiasm for dating that is entertaining to listen to and leaves me a little breathless. *Is this what I sounded like in the zenith of my dating prowess?* I wonder. She often wants to talk about her lesbian identity—like, she's *really* fucking excited about it. I don't think I've ever had such long conversations about being a dyke before, even when that's what I was perceived to be, even when that was the default identity that felt better than anything else I could possibly conceive of for myself. *Butch* was an apartment I could fit most of myself into and live happily for a little while. But she is so happy to be a lesbian. I think if the politics around Michfest hadn't been so fucked up, she would have been over the moon there. That shit was *made* for a woman like Brook. She belongs.

A WHILE BACK, a trans woman in my town was angry at me on social media for performing with Sister Spit, a rotating line-up comprised mostly of queer cis women—but not all—that I'd been involved with in some way for over twenty years. She was tired of feeling like trans men get included in spaces where she doesn't feel included but wants to. She said, "I'm tired of how all the trans men always get a free pass."

Free? I want to joke. *Do you know how many women I had to get off to get here?*

But in all seriousness, I do understand her pain. And she is right: She, too, wants to be embraced in a community of queer women, accepted as a co-conspirator, and from where she's standing, it appears to her that I have the community I always had in my butch past—which isn't accurate, but I can understand how it comes off that way to her. It's still more connection than she feels like she has.

I hate the sense of scarcity that pervades our trans community, the way we are always holding our sharpest knives up toward each other. In her eyes, I am privileged in my dyke history; in my skin, I too long for that sense of community, of belonging. I wish she could see the extent of my *lonesome*, the way I can walk right up to queer women I know in public, only to have them look away until I say hello. As a bearded, precariously-near-middle-age man, I am to be avoided. I am unseen. I miss that feeling of striding into a space to be greeted by the folks in my community. She and I are both outsiders, twirling alone in the sawdust of an empty dance floor. I am sad that we trans folks are often so deep within the cocoons of our own pain that we cannot make refuge for each other.

BROOK READS *Valencia*, which describes circles of people I was running with at that time, and she tells me she is jealous. I tell her stories of my early twenties in dyke-run San Francisco. We didn't really *run* the city so much as we created self-sufficient microcosms within which we could thrive and create. We didn't own anything; we weren't the boss. But the worlds we fabricated with our raw knuckles and greedy mouths stretched a biosphere across the city, or at least it felt like it, and it was easy to imagine that this entire place belonged to queers, a feeling most of us had never had before—or never have had since. We roosted the city, claimed it. We were a noisy murder of crows laughing in the streets, fucking in the alleys, dancing and rocking out in bars, mounting shows in underground performance spaces, hosting orgies and play parties and confessionals in our bedrooms, planting our pirate flag along the bows of playground structures of our city. Every corner held our secrets. Sex was part of our art and we did a lot of both. We came together, our own Left Bank, and we appointed our own Gertrudes and Ernests and Pablos and Alices.

I DISCOVER another word: *saudade ([saw 'dadʒi] or Soh-dah-zgche)*, a Portuguese word that also has no direct corollary in English. It evokes a deep emotional state of nostalgia or profound, melancholic longing for an absent object of one's love—an object of love that doesn't necessarily need to be romantic or even a person. The sense that the longed-for may be long gone is tamped down in the ashy bottom of one's heart. We pave over that ache with denial of the inevitable. The less one is sure of the missing target's whereabouts, this yearned-for someone or something, the stronger this feeling will be.

Saudade might describe the pangs of hope of the widow in her watch, always scanning the crease between sky and sea. *Saudade* perhaps describes the negative space, the hollow in your sheets that once housed your lover's warmth. While remembering an estranged lover with whom you never got to reconcile, *saudade* might speak to the pang of desire that survives in the desert of a dozen empty years between she and you. *Saudade* might be your reluctance to let go of that long-lost love, because in doing so, you will have to finally relinquish childish love and learn how to love like a grown man. I may be projecting my shit onto this beautiful word. But it's even more complicated, for *saudade* also means we find some pleasure, perhaps even joy within our wistful ache. This isn't quite the right word Brook was looking for either, but I think I'm getting warmer.

I'm gifted two tickets to an L7 reunion show, and of

course I can't think of a better sidekick to take than Brook. I joke about how it's like a retirement party for old punk queers, and I have a fucking blast despite my aching back and exhaustion. I want Brook to be included in a world of badass women that no longer includes me. I tell her about the time, long ago, that I fisted a coworker for an art film, talked into it both in the name of art and for the anonymity that was later blown on the big screen by my easily recognizable elbow tattoos. I want to take her to dance at Junk at the Stud, and to see Tribe 8 play at the Covered Wagon Saloon. I want to drag her down to the subterranean Coco Club and get her to sign up on the Sister Spit open mic list. I tell her about the dyke-owned cafe I worked at as a short-order cook, of weekend brunch rushes where we'd have the countertop seated shoulder-to-shoulder with hot queer women who ogled us as we sizzled up their food and plopped it onto thick, porcelain diner plates, and how we loved every minute of our objectification under their hungry eyes, how we came alive in the glow of it. But more than any of this, I want Brook to find her own place, in her own time, with her own peers, a place of queer futurity that can only exist in this present moment with *her* in it.

I WANT to teach my friend about a past that I loved but wasn't fully mine, a gorgeous vintage shirt that hangs in your closet, full of stories but never fits you quite right, at least not anymore. A moldering box of photographs carried from place to place. I want to teach my friend about a time that at least part of me felt at home and welcomed, a place where I could express some of my gender and still be loved in it. I want to bequeath this complicated playground to her, even though it's not mine to give and continues to turn to mulch beneath the more expensive heels of those who stomp those streets now, no longer in search of art or sex but of gelato and artisanal tacos. The grit of our history is burnished into the pavement beneath the wheels of a monolithic tech company bus.

My inclusion there was always conditional, so long as I played a part, stayed an erotic placeholder, kept my mouth shut. I kicked myself out before anyone else had a chance to exclude me. I might have stayed and subjected myself to the vulnerable ordeal of allowing myself to be known, of allowing others to witness my growth. I robbed myself of that. Taking off was a survival skill I learned early on. There is much I lost in my itinerancy, my wandering alone in the desert while I transitioned. There's something to be said for staying put and tending to your roots.

"Some things you lose, some things you give away."
—SLEATER-KINNEY, "GOOD THINGS"

I tell Brook about my time in this world, because she wants to know. I can be her eyes on the ground of the past. I want to share with B the class notes of a course I aced, even though it was never going to be my major. I want to share with her the films I watched in the early dawning of my conscious desire for women, the films that didn't quite reflect the interstices of my own desires and embodiment, but were an imperfect *something*. It's something like a wave that you return, until you realize it was for the person standing behind you—not intended for you, but a friendly gesture nevertheless.

I propose a late '80s, early '90s formative dyke film fest where we watch *The Hunger*, *Reform School Girls*, *Go Fish*, and *Bound*. I imagine us laughing our asses off to Jennifer Tilly's amazing line, "I have a tattoo . . . would you like to see it?" Back then, the depiction of butch/femme in *Bound* made us laugh uncomfortably from the red velvet seats of the Castro Theater during the premiere screening, but despite the plucked eyebrows on the butch, it was closer to us than we could've imagined seeing on-screen at that time. We, too, imagined ourselves the noble outlaws, the ones who could get away with the money and the girl.

I WANT to tell my friend about the time I was living as a butch-of-sorts, how I was seen as a mannish woman and how there was joy to be found there for me, even if it was a wave intended for the person standing near me—how even street violence and harassment and fists in my face and security guards pulling me out of restrooms only made me stronger in my resolve not to bow to anyone. I want to say how I was like Cool Hand Luke and I just kept getting back up; I want to make it sound like I was tougher than I really was. I want to confess that it is so much easier for me to own my girlhood of sorts, now that I am no longer bound by it— that I had to get *here* to be brave enough to see and love my own past selves.

And sometimes I want to ask my friend about the boyhood she never inhabited but that I never got to have, whether it felt like a friendly gesture intended for the person standing behind her, whether there were things she loved and things she hated, whether she is grateful for the pain because it shaped the woman she can now be. I want our childhood selves to go back in time, to meet and plant a seed of being seen. I want our adult selves to whisper in each other's kid ears that in the future, we won't be switching sides; there is no point A to point B, no train heading west while another heads east, no golden spike in the middle. We will whisper inaudible words while slowly tracing a spiral on each other's backs with our fingertips. There will be no adjoining gurneys where parts are swapped. We will each arrive someday as our own Pygmalion, carving our own forms the best we can from our own material and imaginations.

"The concept [of saudade*] has many definitions, including a melancholy nostalgia for something that perhaps has not even happened. It often carries an assurance that this thing you feel nostalgic for will never happen again."*
—JASMINE GARSD, NPR

I can laugh at myself and my melancholic lament. I am such a different person, as anyone would be, close to two decades after my twenties, and I would never want to go back. Even on my dark days, I'm committed to the adventure of living and finding out what comes next. I don't regret transitioning or the choices I've made, even the choices I made when I didn't realize I had a choice. But I do miss that sense of easy belonging, the vibrancy and generosity of community, the playfulness and the trickster resilience of then. The swagger and spit and ferocity. The way we all found ourselves tossed together there, in this one time and place. I want Brook to feel that sense of belonging, a queer woman among other queer women, some of who might not be women, some of whom are not women yet, some of whom were always guys who felt at home with us, some who might leave queer identity behind altogether like a thrifted sequin gown on a lover's chipped-paint, hardwood floor.

I want to hand over the keys to a kingdom I no longer have, left on my couch after a sweaty tussle, never really gifted to me, the hesitant occupancy of a dog that is suspected of having the capacity to bite and therefore betray. *How can I give her something that was only conditionally mine, but that I love like it was my own?* I find myself in the role of an unlikely link, coupling her to a slice of dyke life that is foreclosed to me. I imagine us together, brokering a peace deal among warring nations and trying to convey the lives that would be saved when non-trans women welcome and protect trans women. I imagine that noisy rookery in the high branches, the cackling of joy, the return to that old punk, dyke, fuck-you spirit that saved my life and can still save lives for those who need it.

Antoinette, for Example

Everybody was so nonchalant about gender, except for me. Perhaps there should've been a big, blaring *I AM TRANS* sign in blue and red neon tubing that blurs to purple in the rain, blinking above the edifice of my obvious, open-24/7 problem with gender. That's why I'd get so pissed I'd almost spit my spirit-gummed mustache off when someone called me a drag king. Why the ratcheted-tight, breath-harnessing ace bandage squeezing my rib cage always felt like a referendum from God, rather than a temporary means to the end of boobs.

Take Antoinette, for example. We are introduced at a party in the third-floor flat of Javier and Chuy, two gay boys we each adore. The Castro is thumping away just around the corner like the heart of a chased gazelle, and the fog hangs low, swaddling the streets, and now we can remember that we live right next to the sea. Chuy introduces me to Antoinette and she barnacles herself onto me, having started the party a couple of hours sooner. Her forearm hangs casually through my elbow and across my forearm like I've belonged to her my whole life—easy, familiar, affectionate. It sparks up where her smooth skin meets the top of my arm.

It's the mid-1990s, so naturally she's wearing a latex dress as tight and red as a birthday balloon, and really, she does the outfit justice. Her lips are painted red to match, her pale skin, black eyes, and black hair popping in contrast to the dress, and when she sits on the stuffed arm of the chair she's just spooned me into without effort, the dress makes a basketball-court-sneaker-squeak between the upholstery and her ass. She swings a leg across my lap, fastening me into the seat like the gate to a roller coaster car. She sips the drink she hasn't spilled a drop of this entire time.

Antoinette may be drunk, but she exudes poise. Me, I'm as dressed up as I tend to get, in my favorite embroidered Western shirt and unwashed 501s, rough as sandpaper, and big, black boots worn-down in the heels. A ubiquitous ball cap curved and salt-greasy shoved down over my brow to hide the constant surprise and innocence of my face. I dress like a white stereotype of something I've never been, my mid-twenties face telegraphing how I'm a girl playing at being a man, how badly I want to evolve into an adult. If I pull my hat brim down just a tiny bit lower, it might hide my hunger for the attention of women, how I long to be claimed—to be adored despite my affliction of butchness, my smell of *other*. The seriousness of my gender stiffens my gait, levels my shoulders to square, makes me look behind myself on the street.

Then Antoinette's red-encased form pools down onto me in the chair, and her hand slips up the back of my neck, beneath the fringe of curls that escapes my hat. Her fingers furrow rows in my hair, and I feel this everywhere in a body I spend a lot of time outside of.

The party swirls around us, glasses and bottles, cadences of laughter and loud talking and three-fourths of the attendees trying to squeeze into the comforting, yellow crush of the kitchen. Someone flips the records and Antoinette and I float alone on an iceberg in the middle of the living room. She's telling me a funny story about her beloved-but-strict Korean parents, and I wonder what it would be like to be worthy of her. She seems so whole, untainted. I imagine my damage to be a kite digging its point in the grass, something that all of her happiness would never manage to hoist aloft. The painted petals of her lips graze my ear, so close I can smell her lipstick. I want to taste it on my teeth.

Out of nowhere, Antoinette says, "When I'm, like, fifty years old, I'll totally transition to male. Why not? I'd like to spend half of my life as a woman, and the rest as a man. I think that'd be interesting." She looks at my face, inert as a medicine ball, and she laughs. Not at me. She's not a dick, I'm sure of this. But the sheer depth of her laugh, the way it travels from somewhere far below her diaphragm, the way it beaches our ice floe onto the shores of the living room carpet so that everyone at the party remembers we are there, the joy of it—I know it's teaching me something I'm not yet ready to understand. I lay a slip of paper here, bookmark it in my memory.

A COUPLE of weeks from now, we'll go on a date. Antoinette will treat me to a Doc Watson concert; she shares my love of Americana. She'll drive us in a 1968 Mustang the color of sweet cream. When I compliment her car, she'll tell me it's a gift from her slave, her most regular client. She's cheerful about everything, and I'll feel exposed by the lightness of her. On our second date, she'll come over to the apartment in the Mission where I'm couch-surfing and hang out with me and watch *G.I. Jane* on VHS. My dog will be recuperating from getting spayed and I won't want to leave her because she'll be nauseous from being put under. She'll be curled up in a ball on her bed to hide her shaved and sutured belly. We'll watch Demi Moore sweating, doing crazy sit-ups and push-ups, shaving her head. It'll be kind of hot.

Antoinette will say the movie inspires her, gives her ideas for scenes at work. There, Antoinette is the boss, called "Mistress" by the men who pay; the first time naked beneath me, she'll call me "daddy." It will surprise me, because I'll feel as fragile and stitched-together as my dog. And I'll think, *I don't know about all that.* I don't even have a place to live.

NOW THE party winds down, and Antoinette insists that I get her home. The boys hug us and wink at me. I catch her arm as her high heel snags the carpet of the stairs, before she slips all the way down. I fasten my leather jacket and helmet onto her, cocoon her in my too-big armor. She straddles my bike behind me, drunk and listing, not easy in the latex. I hope I don't get pulled over, helmetless, as I drive her to her apartment door seven blocks away. Antoinette's arms coil around my belly and she sings and sways as I roll through the streets turned unfamiliar and mysterious by the blanket of fog. I see her through her door, and her red lips stick to mine briefly. She starts to pull me in.

I don't want to be alone, but I want to face another even less. I turn away, back down into the low gloom. The headlight of my motorcycle punches a small hole of clarity through the damp veil hanging thick in the streets around me.

Car Crash on Interstate 5

You know when it's raining so hard that you can't see, and your windshield wipers aren't doing anything? I'm almost back to Portland, about an hour away in Washington on I-5 South, and I see vehicles pulled over. People are standing outside of their cars in the dumping rain, waving their arms like they're snuffing out a fire with a blanket. Flagging me down.

I look to the median. There's an SUV completely flipped over onto its roof, crushed up against the jersey barrier.

Without even thinking about it, I pull my truck over, flip on the hazards, and run across I-5. I try to open the doors, but I can't. The airbags, deployed in the crash, are pushed up against the windows, so it looks like a giant marshmallow has exploded inside the car. I can't see the people. It's so fucking quiet, even in the deluge.

One of the people who was waving their arms runs across the highway, and he too starts pulling on the doors, trying to open them. We cannot hear a sound from inside.

This man—a short and burly Puerto Rican dude—and I run around this smashed car, pulling on the doors. We yell, "Pop the locks! Pop the locks!"

Nothing happens.

My adrenaline starts to scream static through my ears. Another guy comes over, a white construction guy wearing an orange reflective vest. He kneels down and yells at the car, "Are you hurt? How many people? Help is coming!"

I point straight at him and say, "Call 911." You know that thing? They tell you that if you need someone to call 911, you have to point at a specific person and demand that they make the call: *You! White construction guy! Call 911!* You can't just say, *Somebody call 911!* Otherwise, everybody will be like, *Oh, man, I thought you did it. No, I thought you did it.*

SO, construction guy calls 911. In his reflective vest, he slows down traffic, and the short, burly guy and I are trying to get this car open. We try the back hatch together without success, and then he goes to the passenger side. All of a sudden, I hear breaking glass and I run around to the passenger side. In the front passenger door, there's broken glass, and these feet emerge—bare feet. The burly man and I reach down, each taking a foot and gently pulling a woman out of the car. She looks distraught.

We ask her how many other people are in the car. "One," she says in a thick Chinese accent, gesturing. A bald head appears, and two hands.

Burly guy and I pull out a man and ask him if he's okay. He says he's having trouble breathing. He's also barefoot. It's frickin' December. Their bare feet make me think that they were very comfortable on this trip, and very much not expecting to crash and land upside-down in the middle of a freeway.

We quickly check out the Chinese couple, scanning their heads and bodies for injuries, asking them if they're hurt. There's not a scratch on them and they say they're okay, though clearly very shaken and in shock. We can't believe it—somehow, they're fine.

Another guy runs over and shouts, "We've got to get these people out of the middle of the highway. It's not safe for them here. We've got to get them to the shoulder."

I tell him, "They're barefoot, we've gotta carry them." I'm thinking about broken glass, sharp twists of metal on wet asphalt. So I scoop the man up and run across I-5, carrying him in my arms. Construction dude lifts up the woman, and he runs across the highway with her.

I hear a lot of stories about trans people needing to be saved, needing to be rescued. And I just want you to know, you never fucking know—one day, one of us might be carrying you across I-5 from the wreckage of your car. *I'm just saying.*

So, we're across the highway with these barefoot people in our arms, and it feels so scary—like the end of the world, somehow, but all the semi-trucks are approaching really,

really slow. It's like everybody gets it; everybody is going ten miles an hour down the highway. Moving with care for others. We put the people down, and then we're all just standing there like, *What do we do now?*

Someone offers, "Hey, do you want to come sit inside my car to get warm?"

And the people say "No, thank you." They just keep staring at their crumpled car.

The woman is really upset about it, understandably, and the short, burly guy says to her, "Don't worry about it. That's just stuff. God was protecting you tonight, and you are fine."

She says, "Oh, but my *car*."

And he says gently, "No, it's just stuff. It's just stuff."

They want to wait for the highway patrol to arrive. The man seems better with his breathing, but still shaken. I run to my truck and pull out my flashlight. It's huge, but the batteries are *so* dead. There's just a tiny wink of light, and I use it to flag oncoming traffic while the semis are going by really slow—and then the burly guy comes over to me and puts his arms around me, and he holds me. And I hold him.

And suddenly, we're both crying. He looks me in the eyes and says, "God was speaking to you tonight." Even though he's like six inches shorter than me, he envelopes both my hands in his huge, sandpapery hands. "God bless you."

I said: "God bless *you*."

I know it's not very cool to talk about God in Portland, and I'm not religious at all—I'm a fucking Buddhist. But having been raised Catholic, getting my sacraments and doing my time in Saint Bridget's Church, I'm not unfamiliar with such talk.

Like he knows all of this about me on some intrinsic, psychic level, he says again, "God was speaking to you tonight. Even if you didn't know what he was saying, you heard him. You heard him." And I think, *I often don't know what it is that god, or the goddess, or spirit, or the ghost of my dead brother, is trying to tell me.*

He and I are standing there in the rain on the shoulder of the highway, looking at each other and crying. Then he holds his right hand up and I see that his knuckles are swollen, raw, and bloody. He makes a gesture of pain and then a striking motion with his fist, and I understand now that he smashed the passenger window with his bare hand so that the people could escape the wreck.

And then the fire trucks come, and the ambulance comes, and the firefighters look at us gathered around the people from the crashed car. They say, "Well, it was very nice of you people to stand here and wait around, but it's time to clear the traffic."

We all look at each other quizzically, the actual rescuers, like, *Uh, oh okay, see ya.* None of us bother to say, "Well, we pulled them out of the wreck—you're welcome." Instead, I say goodbye to the man and woman from the car, and the man hugs me. They speak to the firefighters in heavy accents.

I say to one of the firefighters, "You have to make sure

to get these people home." The firefighter assures me that the troopers would get them home safely. Then, we all shake hands, and construction guy says, "Merry Christmas," and we all get into our vehicles and take off into the dark rain.

I call my partner on the phone and tell her I love her, and I cry. She keeps asking, "Are you okay?" and I keep saying, "Everyone is okay."

RECENTLY, my friend Michelle Tea, was speaking here in town, and somebody from the audience asked her a question about activism. And she said, "Well, I think the most important thing to ask is 'What can I do that's helpful?'"

It's that simple. Like, what is helpful *right now*? I wanted to tell this story because I think over the next few years, we're going to have to listen extra hard for when God* is speaking to us, and we're going to have to be really helpful. I've thought a lot about all of this over the last two years—about what that guy who broke out the window said to me on the side of the road, and what it actually means. And to me, in that moment, what it meant to be spoken to by God was this idea that something mattered more than I did, you know? Something was more important than me, and I didn't think about it. I just did it.

---

*Or whatever you want to call spirit, collective consciousness, source, your sense of humanity, the goddess, higher power, etc.

Soil, Shit, and Compost

"Self-transformation is precisely what life is."
—RAINER MARIA RILKE

I once thought, for many reasons, that a Buddhist path was closed to me. I'd long held the betrayal and rejection of my youth by a church that purported to speak of Christ's endless love muttered a message out of the other side of its mouth. Everyone else could come in for a weekly purge of their sins, but people like me were a centrifuge of wrongness that could never be washed clean. I remember that feeling of being severed from spirit so clearly, pinching off that electric current that once pulled me up and out of my skin, stitched me to the sky, made me feel the tug of something greater than—outside of—ourselves. The web of God attached its tentative fiber to my body, the voltage of love vibrated between me and all of Creation, and a neon light of spirit flickered bright in my chest. The words of men, not God, were all that it took to cut me loose from everything.

Hypocrisy slowly filled the cup of me, displacing the euphoria of God's love with the condemnation of God's followers as my physical form continued to evolve outside of the lines sketched out for me. "Do not be bewildered by the surfaces; in the depths all becomes law," Rilke advised his mentee, a young poet, in the early 1900s.[1] I wish I had known how to plunge into the depths back then, but as anyone who doesn't toe a cultural gender line well knows, the surfaces always reflect your wrongness back at you. Early on, the message seemed clear: *To live in this body meant that there were many important things I stood to lose.*

I also thought I couldn't be Buddhist because I'm not a joiner—all my life, I've resisted joining. Tell me we all have to do a thing and I turn the other way; to define is to hem in, to limit. It was the way in which definitions and labels were foisted upon me from such a young age: *Catholic. Girl. Weirdo. Man. Slut. Gay. Freak. Fuck-up.*

In the late 1980s, my very first girlfriend loaned me a copy of Chögyam Trungpa Rinpoche's *Meditation in Action* and took me to see HH the Dalai Lama speak in a vast conference hall in Boston. I felt immediate trepidation and an inexplicable pull while flipping through the slim volume, inhaling the scents of espresso and Nag Champa incense that imbued the book from its tenure on the shelves of Trident Bookstore Café on Newbury Street. It was here that my burgeoning queerness, transness, and a yearning for clarity and spiritual anchor began an inchoate intertwine.

I tried to study *Meditation in Action*, only to be confronted with my inability not only to sit still, but to also read about sitting still. Just reading about mindfulness back then asked of me a level of mindfulness I'd yet to possess. I'd fashioned myself into a spiky sea urchin to protect my soft places. Things happened *around* me and *to* me; convinced I could feel it all, I responded in kind, tossed about on whitecaps of uncut emotion, unable to see any way I could plot my own course.

I misunderstood, thinking that the teachings of the Buddha asked of me perfection from the outset, but I was wrong. The church taught me that I was born wrong, and that my life would be an endless tide chart of accrued sins that I could attempt to scour away with the high pressure-wash of confession and a battery of Our Fathers and Hail Marys.

"One cannot really start by being perfect," Chögyam Trungpa Rinpoche taught, "but one must start with something."[2] I wasn't quite ready to accept that perhaps who and what and where I was, *was* exactly the something I needed to start with. The Buddha cautioned followers to not do what he said just because he said it, but to see if he was right by testing his teachings out for themselves.

Funny how I still resist defining my spirituality even now, when I understand that a sangha is a siblinghood of spiritual anarchists.

Another reason I thought I couldn't be a Buddhist was because of my ancestral inheritance of chaos and anger. I believed that a life of the mind, of contemplation and grace, was foreclosed to me by the violence of my childhood and the turmoil of my life thereafter. I was a wild, feral thing;

my anger and my love were equally explosive. I learned by failing at how to be right: in the world, in relationship. I was certain that I was not worthy.

During the mid-1990s, when I was in my twenties, I took a job as a cook at Maitri AIDS Hospice, which was then part of the Hartford Street Zen Center in San Francisco. The hospice was started by Issan Dorsey, the acting spiritual director at Hartford Street, and its mission was to house gay men who were dying of AIDS on the streets. I wanted to care for people living with and dying from AIDS, having recently lost a partner to the disease myself. In the early 1990s, a diagnosis was still most likely a death sentence, and so many of us were fatigued by chronic grief and the endless stream of loss: of lovers, friends, mentors, heroes, community members. I was young, confused, enraged—an emotional cripple. I hadn't been there at the very end when my lover passed, hadn't been able to be there, and the fact of this consumed me with grief and remorse in equal measure. Making meals for the dying was both an act of learning to bear witness and my self-imposed penance.

My lover had eroded away—it was shocking to see how much one could lose and still remain alive. I saw glimpses of her in the hollow cheeks and sharp shoulders of the residents sometimes, and the way the illness made the fire of a person's eyes seem to glow fiercer for the bleakness surrounding them. "Often it seems as if there is no body at all, only bare phenomena dissolving away continuously,"

Sayadaw U Pandita says. "One cannot unsee nor disremember the disintegration of a human life."[3]

I remember mentioning to a kitchen volunteer one day that I was interested in sitting with the others in the basement Zendo sometime, but that I was too angry a person for meditation.

"The Buddha teaches us that it is okay to have that anger within us," the volunteer replied, as he whacked apart carrots with the silver flash of a chef's blade.

A former girlfriend's father, a man who'd cultivated a regular meditation practice in his middle age, once told her, "Look, people don't become Buddhists because they *already* have inner peace."

Chögyam Trungpa Rinpoche said that divesting ourselves of our self-criticism can unroot us, since it has become something of a livelihood, and to lose that is to feel like we've lost our job. Truly, we can make a career out of shitting on ourselves. He says that "trying to be calm, trying to be good, is also an aspect of striving, of neuroticism."

Most of all, I never thought I could be a Buddhist because I needed to change my body. It once seemed antithetical to me to try to be both trans and Buddhist. Buddhists are all about the impermanence of everything, and of course trans people are all about carving out a home in one's own temporary, fleeting skin. But nothing allows for a sense of nonattachment, of impermanence and of letting go, quite like gender transition, which by its own name evokes movement, of always becoming, of a leap away from the static. Nothing has ever made me more aware of all that I could not control more so than transition, and by being able to experience the relief of being "in" my own body, I could allow the barriers between myself and others to dissolve.

In the New Testament, the first epistle to the Thessalonians says, "Every one of you should know how to possess his vessel in sanctification and honor." Are our bodies not our vessels? Rilke's letters on love speak to the idea that we must possess our own selves "to be able to find a way out of ourselves, out of the depth of [our] already shattered solitude." Both ideas speak to the notion that our bodies are necessary vehicles to connection with both mind and spirit, and are what make us not-separate from others. As I was able to embrace and forgive my own vulnerability, I was able to embrace and forgive and love the vulnerability of others. Through making friends with myself, I began to make friends with what is.

This winter, I attended a queer Dharma talk at the Portland Shambhala Center entitled "Transformation: No big deal and nothing personal." At first, I imagined that I would want to talk about being trans—wasn't that *my* biggest transformation? *The* biggest transformation? But then I realized that in that context, to emphasize my physical "transformation" would mean to make it about me. I saw that it wasn't the change that was transformative, but the idea that I was okay as I was, that where I was at was where I needed to be.

"Transformation comes from a willingness to grow very slowly and to be whatever life asks of us," teacher Michaela McCormick said during her talk. "Transformation is not about *me*."

"If your reaction to a big loss is only 'what I need,' then you never really leave your cocoon of habitual patterns," said McCormick. I'd been conditioned to see my trans body, transition or not, as flawed and wrong. And meditation is not an escape—there is no escape in life from my body. My trans body's transness is present whether I change my body or not.

Transition gave me a calm in my body from where I could begin to witness the chaos of my mind. My body became a teacher when I was able to finally acknowledge it as mine. By accepting my body's inherent transness, I had to accept my inherent and flawed humanity. I became a human being; now human, I could cultivate compassion for others from an acceptance of our shared humanity. Accepting my body as trans helped me see how much I am like other people—not special or different—because in accepting my body I had to accept life and the fact that I was living it. Quieting the chaos of my division, my internal fractures, helped me let go of the false story of my aloneness. From the quiet, I began to tear free from within my cocoon.

Chögyam Trungpa Rinpoche said, "The opposite of self-deception is just working with the facts of life." One of the facts of my life is that my body is trans, and that in order to live my life, I had to accept that I needed to change it. Changing my body wasn't a way out, it was a way *in*.

If we are to follow the Buddha's teachings on dependent origination, of cause and effect, the effect of my transness is not separate of me, of my body, of my mind, or of anything or anyone else. Transition was a process by which I made peace with the body to make friends with the mind, to be able to sit still inside this skin. Being in my body, making peace with the fact that this is the reality of my body, rolled the stone away from the mouth of the cave of my empathy.

"Our body becomes completely useless when we die. What use can one make of a corpse?" Sayadaw U Pandita asks. "The body is like a very fragile container that can be used as long as it is intact, but the moment it drops on the floor, it is of no further help to us."

Having a healthy body gives us the means to practice. Without a body, we cannot sit. Trungpa Rinpoche teaches of the interdependence of form and spaciousness: ". . . in order to experience open space one also must experience the solidity of earth, of form." We must understand our six sense doors to learn the power to be found in sense restraint. Transition was a path for me to understand the sense door of my body.

Sayadaw U Pandita speaks of the need to care for and to keep clean one's internal base—the body and one's external base, the home. "When the eyes fall upon dirt and untidiness, mental confusion tends to arise, but if an environment is clean, the mind becomes bright and clear. This mental state is ideally conducive to the development of wisdom." Similarly, transition was a way in which I was able to create order and cohesion in my life.

Trungpa Rinpoche has called our histories as sentient beings the fertile soil in which we can begin to cultivate wisdom, even if ugly, stupid, violent, or ignorant:

> We do not have to be ashamed of what we are. As sentient beings we have wonderful backgrounds. These backgrounds may not be particularly enlightened or peaceful or intelligent. Nevertheless, we have soil good enough to cultivate; we can plant anything in it.

There's a saying that an unskillful farmer will pay someone to haul away her animals' shit, while a skillful farmer will save her manure, tend it, and allow it to decompose into rich fertilizer, with which she can enrich her soil and feed her crops. The stuff with which we already sit down is the rich shit we can try to squirm away from in discomfort, or that we can hang out with and tap for all of the wonderful compost our experiences provide. This sentiment is echoed by Sayadaw U Pandita, who writes, "From this rubbish heap we call our body, we can nonetheless extract gold through the practice of the Dhamma."

Some might say that figuring out I was trans would in itself be a desire to change, but to me, it was an acceptance of what I already was: a trans body that could either be accepted or not accepted, that I could choose to know or to ignore. The path of denying what I was felt more arduous and perilous, even though the thought of changing something as radical as my physical form was overwhelming.

The basic meditation practice I first learned was to see what is, to wipe the grime free of the lens of my mind's eye. At first, I'd sit and be astonished by the acrobatics my mind would drill through to avoid stillness. The thin, toothy blade of my whipsaw mind bows and whistles as I run to be the lumberjack pulling on each side. I was certain I was a crazy person. Now, I think that I am *probably* a crazy person, but I get to sit here in dignity anyway.

I can see the relationship between my practice as an artist and my mediation practice. When I wake up some mornings to my whipsaw mind already chipping through my day, I can sit and meditate and bring a bit of sanity back to my life. My dear friend Anna Joy told me that all that meditating sure takes up a lot of time, but it actually gives us back all the time we'd otherwise waste on being crazy. I think of her every time I halt a scrambled-mind meltdown by setting my timer and dropping my ass down on the cushion. A short pause can bellow out the tight folds of my day.

It is perhaps the sense of being separate from others, and also not ready or worthy to undertake practice that Trungpa Rinpoche spoke of when he cautioned against spiritual materialism. He writes of a metaphorical monkey caught in a wheel of samsara, who comes to realize that the barriers imprisoning his life were based on an imagined false dichotomy of him versus others. His notion of self, cleaved apart from the world, was a rampart of his own creation. "And so he begins to realize," Trungpa Rinpoche teaches, "that to be free of his prison he must give up his ambition to escape and accept the walls as they are." And in this way, I accept my trans body as it was, as it is, and as it will be.

Notes

1. Rainer Maria Rilke, *Letters to a Young Poet* (New York City: W. W. Norton & Company, 1993).
2. Chögyam Rinpoche Trungpa, *Meditation in Action* (Boulder: Shambhala Publications, 2010).
3. Sayadaw U. Pandita, *In This Very Life: Liberation Teachings of the Buddha* (Boston: Wisdom Publications, 1992).

Half as Sensitive

It was never my dream to get a job where I had to wear a uniform, patrol a campus, and worry about getting jumped or shot by methed-out burglars; or worse—every shift I risk getting puked on, doused in glitter, or hugged by a naked person painted completely blue. The uniform becomes another layer of my in-between, makes my visible invisible, makes my invisible illegible, a message scribed in sand with a stick, rubbed out before the waves can pull the words away. I leave my life as a teacher and writer and assume the costume of a professional scold on a campus that would otherwise be unlikely to have me.

I ENTER and perform a security check on the reactor core at least once, and often up to three times per shift. A small, plain, gray concrete building houses the facility at the college where I work as a campus safety officer. There is a secure bay with a twenty-five-foot-deep "swimming pool" that cools the reactor with water. That spooky blue glow you see in pictures, Cherenkov radiation, is not visible when I'm inside. In fact, I'm not certain whether the reactor is even running or not. I check a few safety details, and the security of the area. The main thing is to ensure the cooling water is at a visible level. Children's mylar pinwheels turn lazy circles in the wall vents, indicating airflow. Turns out there are thirty-one such "non-power" or research reactors across the United States.

IT'S RATHER underwhelming to be inside this nuclear reactor. When I first started the security job, I imagined it might be otherwise. Back when I lived in New Mexico, people still spoke of the wildfire that burned the edges of the Los Alamos National Laboratory, just over a ridge of the Sangre de Christos from where I worked. One day on *Democracy Now*, Amy Goodman said that if New Mexico seceded from the US, it would be the third largest nuclear power in the world. The echoes of the atomic age are still stitched into the land, visible on street signs, still employing thousands of people. I've never found anything more frightening than the unstoppable drive toward the invisible, annihilating potential of the nuclear. I grew up watching Saturday afternoon movies on Channel 56 Boston's *Creature Double Feature*, my mind filled with the black-and-white monstrosities that haunted the Japanese after Hiroshima. *Godzilla was our fault. Matango: Attack of the Mushroom People* haunted me in particular. To find myself inside a nuclear reactor on a frequent basis is, to say the least, an unexpected twist.

ALONG THE bank of the Columbia River in the southeastern corner of Washington State, 200 miles from where I work, the Hanford Nuclear Site kept a laboratory near the F Reactor for testing the effects of radiation on animals. It was called, with a banality specific to the federal government, the 100F-55 Experimental Animal Farm (or EAF). Between 1961 and 1964, the scientists kept up to fifty-five alligators there. They were kept in a pen warmed with sun lamps and equipped with a small pond. The scientists liked to play with them and feed them trout. In tests and experiments, forty-five alligators were exposed to radiation doses—roentgens—and ten were kept as control animals. During observation periods they found the radiation caused damage to the alligators' small intestines and their hematopoietic, or blood-forming, systems. For other species, these effects occur quickly after exposure, but for the alligators, the damages did not become apparent until the second month after exposure. This tipped the scientists off to the possibility that a lower body-temperature might forestall the impact of radiation exposure.

I FIRST learned of the irradiated alligators by chance, an offhand oddity mentioned in an article written by someone who'd illegally hiked the outlying areas of Hanford and noted the way that the landscape, after so many years, seem to be forgiving the abuse humans had leveled upon it. I began to chase the distant twinkle of an obsession. I wanted to find the alligators.

MOST OF the security shifts are defined by an ardent dullness and lots of walking. I let my phone track my steps until the numbers just graphed toward the ridiculous. I walk empty hallways in the science building trying to tap out stabs at poetry with the notes app on my phone. There are long, cold hours in the middle of the night when even the wildest students sleep. I hear—and see—coyotes and three types of owls. I push away the night's encroachment in my mind, replaying obsessions to keep myself awake. To keep the dark at bay.

THE UNITED STATES initiated its atomic bomb program in 1939 because of rumors that the Nazis were developing one. The plutonium for the Manhattan Project was produced at Hanford. The first atomic bomb, the creation of the project, detonated at the test site in between Socorro and Alamogordo, New Mexico. "Trinity" was the code name for the explosion. The rule of three. Three is the magic number. Father, son, and the holy spirit. When I lived in New Mexico, it was said that should the state recede from the nation, it would be the world's third largest nuclear power. New Mexico is steeped in witchy Catholicism, everywhere the Virgen de Guadalupe looms from mission churches, murals, and statuary; radiating from the power of her corona, stomping on a snake.

WEARING A uniform for money renders you either beneath detection, or renders you a target for people's authority issues. But when students get all up on how I am an authority figure, a representation of The Man, all I can think is: *You've never actually had an encounter with real police, have you?*

IN 2011, Hanford scientists discovered a wild rabbit along the brown grassy plains that was contaminated with high levels of radioactive cesium. Wildlife cannot petition for restitution or file a lawsuit. Animals do not complain. Wildlife is a harbinger of bleak portents.

OR ELSE I think: *If only you understood how little authority we actually have.* The real cops and paramedics see us as posers, rent-a-cops. The folks around campus project the reality that suits their present needs on us like we are blank walls, never seeing us as equally human. Really, a security guard is like the blue-collar equivalent of a bisexual—no one on either side sees you as "real." I think about my life as trans and how many years I spent proving myself as real to some authority so that I could just live.

AT ONE point, a bunch of the Hanford alligators escaped. They dug under the chain-link fence and worked their leathery bodies through plywood paneling encircling the man-made gator pond. The scientists followed their tracks in the sand to the Columbia River. One alligator was captured by a fisherman a few months later about nine miles downriver from the nuclear reservation. He had it made into taxidermy. General Electric, the contractor for the facility at the time, confiscated his trophy from a local fishing shop.

SMALL SAMPLES for radiation testing in the reactor pool are packed into tiny capsules called "rabbits."

ONE AFTERNOON, I walk through the crowd of reveling liberal arts students, attempting to discern the TNT-equivalent yield of glitter-bombs (blown-out eggshells filled with glitter and then sealed—these people aren't fucking around). I mentally calculate the ballistic coefficient of projectile vomit. I move on my toes like a ninja, ready to duck and roll away from danger. It's the rite of passage, this bacchanal, for the graduating students. On this day, I am hugged, thanked. We celebrate their passage from the cocoon and on this day, a human inhabits my uniform.

HANFORD HAD banal nicknames for everything. The reactors were known as "piles," and the plutonium separation facilities were "canyons." They called uranium "metal" and weapons-grade plutonium "product." It makes sense that code names were used during the Manhattan Project and the Cold War, but a vernacular of obfuscation lingers around the nuclear even still. These stale codes function as a beard, a disguise, as if diminution of the enormity of power can be afforded by benign words.

HANFORD PRODUCED the product for the Fat Man, the nuclear bomb detonated over Nagasaki in 1945. The bomb killed approximately 40,000 people instantly. Thousands more later, sickness, skin peeling off like birch bark. A city, and then a loud, hot-white nothing. Skeletons of trees jab the gray sky. Something so terrible that it made shadows work in reverse, silhouettes painted in white where cool black used to be. Everything ash, bodies crumbled charcoal sticks.

OKAY, some people on campus engage with the security team as real human beings. Example: the janitorial staff. They are from various Asian countries, mostly Vietnam. All night they clean up puke and broken glass and blood and trash. And glitter. They buff the floors with wax until they shine like warm shallow puddles. The janitorial staff chats and high-fives and laughs with me in the hallways in the middle of the night. One woman stops her mopping to chat, laughing and smacking my upper arm lightly. She tells me that working this job put her two sons through college. Her accent is very heavy, and I don't always understand her the first time. If I listen carefully to the cadence of her words, I can usually shake out points of American English from the music of her speech. She doesn't always understand me, either. We sometimes repeat ourselves a few times. We talk slower, more gently, bring our hands into the exchange, until we craft a makeshift comprehension in the air between us. I look forward to my Friday evening patrol, when we chat for a minute as she finishes up her work for the week and my night is only beginning. The janitors never complain. Not like me. They just do their work, cleaning up other people's messes.

MY LAST NAME: Bombardier. It literally means "bomb thrower" in French. A bombardier is the person responsible for targeting aerial bombs from aircraft. It's also the archaic name for an artillery crewman. I like my name, but it is not exactly the name of a peaceful people. The emotion I saw most frequently expressed growing up was rage. People read my name across the breast of my uniform and tell me what a cool name it is. I don't know how to explain to them the weight of it, or how badly I yearn for peace.

AT THE large annual celebration, the daughter of a famous man chats with me while clutching a bottle of cheap Merlot into her ribcage like a child might hold a favorite stuffed bear. She asks me how I like this particular debauch, and I say it's fine so far, but that I hoped later I wouldn't be finding students with their heads in toilet bowls and with puke in their hair. I say that my primary objective is to make it through the night without being thrown up on or glitter-bombed.

She asks, "If you had to choose between the two, which would you rather?"

I think about this for a moment before responding, "Disgusting as it might sound, I say, I'd rather be puked on than glittered. Puke washes off." She contemplates this for a second, then agrees with a solemn nod.

MY FAMILY is distantly related to the snowmobile Bombardiers. When I was five years old, we visited the Musée Bombardier in Valcourt, Québec. The attendant gave me a complimentary bumblebee-yellow and black snowmobile matchbox car, no doubt after my parents cajoled her into it by telling her we were relatives.

WE TRANSGENDER folks are another lot where the question of realness is pressed down hard from without and wrestled with within. When you are trans, you don't feel "real" in the gender everyone says you are, and when you embark upon transitioning to the gender you know you are, there is the pressure of always wondering if you will ever feel "real enough." To a non-transgender person, it may seem like living as the gender with which you identify is the zenith. But then the rest of your life happens. That's just the made-for-TV happy ending trans people get now that Hollywood knows it's not cool to just portray us as only serial killers. What is missing from this dichotomy is the trade-off of one kind of invisibility for another. As much as anyone longs for another to anoint us as authentic, who but ourselves can decree us "real"?

"FIRE IN THE HOLE."

INSIDE THE reactor, my head aches and my breathing feels somewhat belabored. Probably psychosomatic. The reactor has an odor, too. It smells like what you imagine the inside of such a place to smell like: nothing else you've ever smelled. It smells like science. It smells like the flat, lonely opposite of nature. It smells like a place devoid of the human, a place in which humans are not supposed to be.

To enter the reactor, I have to punch in a personal code, then place the tip of my left index finger on a special pad. The biometric sensor traces the whorls and bifurcations of my fingerprint, and if accepted, the door lock clicks open. The government is giving money to the school to install retinal scanners. Another layer of identity to divine, always problematizing the essence of what makes us real. The future is here. If the Department of Homeland Security can scan my retina here, can it scan it anywhere?

A FINGERPRINT and a nuclear reactor each possess a core.

BOMBARDIER is also a military rank that has existed since the 16th century in artillery regiments of various armies, such as in the British Army and the Royal Prussian Army, instead of the corresponding infantry rank of Corporal. Correspondingly, the rank of Lance-Bombardier is also used instead of Lance-Corporal. I ask my father how this came to be the name of my family as they traced back to Québec and Nova Scotia and generations before that, to the Alsace-Lorraine. He thinks our first ancestor on the paternal side in Canada was a soldier from France. Always fighters.

IN THE novella *Story of the Eye* by Georges Bataille, there is the repeated theme of the orb: the egg, the testicle, the ovum, the eye. But amidst some of the most famously depraved sex scenes in literature, the unnamed narrator finds the sight of a naked, yet shod, person riding a bicycle "irritating and theoretically unclean." I'm with the narrator on this one.

AT THE zenith of its activity, Hanford had nine nuclear reactors. Today, the Hanford River Corridor is one of the United States' biggest environmental clean-up projects. Thousands of tons of radioactive and toxic waste are still being dug up and hauled in trucks to the Waste Isolation Pilot Plant (WIPP) in Carlsbad, New Mexico, about 250 miles away from the original Trinity explosion site at the White Sands Missile Range.

"FIRE IN the hole" is a warning that an explosive detonation in a confined space is imminent.

 PASS WITH CARE

THE CAMPUS security job fell in my lap while I was in grad school. It pays pretty well. It offers health insurance, something elusive in the lives of adjunct professors. It has flexible hours, I can work it around my teaching and writing schedule. I don't see myself doing it forever, but what lasts forever? I check the black water level of the glum, dark pool inside the reactor. The human eye can perceive the eerie luminescence of Cherenkov radiation when charged particles hit the gelatinous cushion of its vitreous humor. So much we think we believe is a function of our ability, or inability, to see.

While I write, the song "Debaser" by the Pixies is playing. Black Francis sings about slicing up eyeballs. He screams again and again: "I am *un chien andalou*." In 1929, just a year after *Story of the Eye* was published, Luis Buñuel and Salvador Dalí released the surrealist film *Un Chien Andalou*. The opening scene features the image of a cloud occluding the moon, then a man slicing a woman's eyeball with a straight razor. The vitreous humour leaks out of her destroyed eye. For the special effect, a calf's eye was used. Like *Story of the Eye*, there are repeated images of a character on a bicycle, and the inevitable focal point of a crash. The bleak notes rung of vision and motion. Blindness and being stuck. The film was supposed to be an exercise in Freudian free-association. Can any association truly be singular or free? I can only see the thin glow of connective tissue, the distant light that nets the constellations together like a ghosted sinew.

MY LIFE is triangulated by "student." I was a graduate student, now a part-time college instructor, and elsewhere, a campus cop. It is an overwhelming trinity, three layers of college roles at once. I am looking forward to break. The campus is spooky when depopulated of students for the summer. Just me and the empty buildings and the screech owls and the stars—each one an incandescent distant orb of light, wrought by nuclear fusion. Each so singular, so far away.

THE ORIGINAL town of Hanford, Washington, a small farming community, was condemned and "depopulated" by the Feds to make way for the nuclear production facility in 1943. Like a bad landlord in a rapidly gentrifying neighborhood, the government served the Hanford people a thirty-day eviction notice, then demolished their homes to make way for something bigger, better, more lucrative. The 100F area of the Hanford Nuclear Reservation is located where the town once stood.

THE BIOMETRIC finger sensor only works if you are warm and alive. No getting in with a cold, dead zombie finger. I learn this the hard way on a particularly cold grave shift. I blow warm breath onto my fingertip, obscuring it for a second before the plume of exhale dissipates into the clear night sky.

AFTER TEACHING a midday college writing class at a state university, I work a shift at the security job from 2:30 in the afternoon to 1:30 the following morning. I shuffle around campus, trying to stay alert and awake. There's another big annual campus event. Outside, a visibly wasted young woman approaches me and the new officer I'm training. She says she's taken some time off from school and doesn't recognize us.

"Who are you guys?"

I introduce myself and my trainee. She wavers in and out of inebriation. She tells me that she's sick of the privileged and entitled attitudes of the student body. She's from a rural town of 4,000 people and she's attending on a full scholarship. She fixes me directly with her big brown eyes, which lock into focus for the first time in this interaction, and then tells me that she's a prostitute. She tells me how empowered she feels, how in control, how she can make two hundred an hour. I don't bat an eye. I just listen.

SCIENTIST Terry Hazen approaches the Hanford clean-up today with a doctrine of infallibility, but not in the Papal sense, where a mortal holy man is cocooned from the ability to commit error. Hazen's doctrine of infallibility asserts that there is no known compound, man-made or natural, that microorganisms cannot degrade. It doesn't waste time trying to account for, or to protect against, human error.

"Bomb" is widely used as an abbreviated form of address for both full bombardiers and lance-bombardiers, as are the informal "full screw" or "lance jack." As with other military vernacular such as "sarge," these terms are not used on formal occasions. When I was a kid, I was often referred to by the nickname "C-bomb."

A FINGERPRINT is topography: crossover, core, bifurcation, ridge-ending, island, delta, pore. Something like a national park in Utah: arch, tentarch, right loop. Left loop, double loop, right pocket loop, left pocket loop, whorl, mixed figure. A microscopic topographical map belonging to you and you alone.

THE STUDENT studies my face for a reaction. My face remains impassive, a tactic I've developed at this job, because while I believe she is telling the truth, her tone indicates that she wishes to impress or shock us. When I was in my twenties, in San Francisco, a good half of my friends and lovers did some manner of sex work, whether working the peep show booth, dancing in strip clubs, pro-domme work, escorting— some even turned outright tricks. We all do what we think we have to do in order to survive. Stars produce their own light through fusion, which happens when lighter elements are forced to become heavier elements. I see a glimpse of the kid beneath her salty veneer, and my blank expression softens. But I say nothing. I remain a body of a man in a uniform.

THE EAF housed up to a thousand different animals at one time. There were sheep, dogs, cows, pigs, and, of course, the alligators. Hanford wasn't the first site to test the effects of radiation on alligators—the Savannah River Site in South Carolina used them prior to Hanford. Alligators can hold their breath for over half an hour, with the longest reported time lasting up to two hours. When the EAF scientists tried to knock out the alligators with ether, they held their breath for a very long time.

THE PHRASE "frag out" is pretty much interchangeable with "fire in the hole."

I JUST nod and listen carefully to the young woman, hoping my unblinking attention bats out some Morse code in reverse that can reveal my empathy or lack of judgment. I am standing there in my uniform, obviously not factoring into her class analysis. I want to imagine that she imagines that I have—and have had—no life, that I am some dumb schlub who works there because I have no other options. But then I see something of how alike we are, tucked into our costumes—the concessions we've made to get what we need, what we've chosen to sell and what we've kept for ourselves, and all the layers of who we really are obfuscated beneath the surface.

AMERICAN ALLIGATORS may live to about fifty years in the

wild, though the Belgrade Zoo in Serbia houses an alligator that is seventy-six years old. After it is four feet long, an alligator is safe from predators except humans and occasionally other alligators. Because they are cold-blooded animals, their body temperatures are determined by their environment.

I DON'T have any stats to back this up, but I would wager a bet that "security guard" would rank amongst the occupations most reviled by others.

ALTHOUGH I was only five at the time of our trip to Québec, I remember playing with a little girl who spoke only French, and her little, black, sweet-piss-smelling puppy, on what seemed like endless, grass-carpeted, rolling hills at a campground where we stayed. I remember the color of sunlight through the faded-blue nylon of the tent. I remember my father speaking fake-French to the teen at a drive-up ice cream bar. He was not attempting to deceive, merely to communicate—hopefully by somehow fitting in. He thought he was asking for a paper bowl, but the boy gave my father a pickled hard-boiled egg instead.

THE FIRST three dozen Hanford alligators were purchased from a farm in Louisiana in 1962. They were young, two to three years old, and they were small: thirty to forty inches in length. Others came from the Okefenokee Swamp. They were kept in a round, concrete fish pond, and in the winter, they were held safe inside a shallow holding tank located in a greenhouse. The round outdoor pond was about thirty inches deep, and to cull reptiles for follow up tests, the technicians pulled on rubber boots and waded through a pool of forty-two snapping creatures. The technicians took to calling this "being up to your ass in alligators." The lead scientists were more concerned about the alligators getting preyed upon by cougars and coyotes than they were concerned about possible escape. They wanted to keep the wild out more than to keep the wild in.

EVEN THOUGH reviled, or sometimes regarded by the students with a tolerating amusement, I am a first-responder on some hairy situations. Life and death shit. The students who get upset when I confiscate a blunt from them have no idea that I might have just saved their buddy's life on the other side of campus only moments before. In order to cope with being both a security guard and a grown (trans) man, I've come to accept that others will feel a need to skip rocks across the surface of who I appear, to them, to be.

A PORTION of the radiobiological experiments carried out at the 100-F EAF involved the use of large animals. The EAF used the animals for studying the potential effects of ionizing radiation exposure to humans in the occupational setting. The Hanford scientists allegedly rubbed the bellies of their test alligators to put them to sleep, since they wouldn't inhale ether. Their smooth, thin, pale-yellow abdomens exposed and vulnerable. Alligators never roll onto their backs by choice, since it causes a sort of vertigo for them. The belly-rubbing bit sounds like bullshit, but then I remember how I used to make lobsters go to sleep by rubbing between their eyes before I dropped them into a stock pot of boiling water many years back when I worked as a line cook.

I THINK about the bombardier, Commander Frederick L. Ashworth, riding along with the Fat Man in the Bockscar over Nagasaki. Hands trembling, or deep-breath calm. The inescapable horror, the unrelenting temptation to find out. The things that can be excused by following orders.

WE DON'T always want to do the work it takes to see to the core of another. Chipping through the accretion of who we are to the vulnerable center: too much. Digging down into the complexity of another person is an overwhelming project. Easier sometimes to simply totalize another, to make pat assumptions, to look only to the surface. We want to stub our toes on the white-blank silhouette of another and stop there. We all clunk around in a uniform or disguise of some kind, whether we want to acknowledge this or not. You gotta give that to the scientists of the EAF: they wanted to look beneath the skin. They wanted to see what was inside.

THE DRUNK, high young woman, perhaps disappointed by my lack of shock, then tells us that she needed to turn to sex work to keep up with the lifestyle of the trust-fund kids. To have the fun, the drugs. Having turned tricks, she now feels that she is capable of anything. Her expression hardens for a note. She says she feels so above all the other students here, but then she says that she likes to be the one who buys all the beer for the party now, so she can contribute. I want to ask her why she wants to buy beer for people she feels so "above" and "over." I want to tell her I get how hard it is to not be seen, to not fit in, to not be accepted. To have to work twice as hard only to be seen as half as good. I get it. Before I find a way to say these things, she has a flicker of coherence and then decides we are no longer her friends.

"So," she says, "you guys are the Authority Figures. You're in charge." The antagonism in her voice is audible.

I want to say to her: *You don't know the half of it, honey*. I want to say to her: *Must be nice to have it all figured out*. I want to say to her: *Is this the best you can do with your radical class analysis—be the working-class kid with a free ride to a college whose annual tuition is more than I have ever earned in a year, is that what you are gonna do, put down blue-collar people who are babysitting your college experience?* I want to say to her: *I get it, it is easier to be combative and sharp than to show another your vulnerability*. To say: *I hurt*.

ONE OF the first experiments with alligators involved a rounded translucent plastic box, bifurcated with a clear divider, an animal on each side nested tail-to-head in their respective partition. This box rotated like a lazy Susan under a large X-ray machine to ensure even, full-body exposure. Placed in a yin-yang of the damned, these animals received high doses of roentgens and died shortly after the experiment. The Hanford scientists in the 1960s surmised that alligators were half as sensitive to radiation as humans.

IN 2003, the F-Reactor was cocooned, entombed in a concrete shroud. It hulks on the dry-grass banks of the Columbia, a gray and white mass, a building boarded up to ward off the storm. Somehow the cocooning makes the reactor appear more ominous in its silence than when it was in operation. What we don't talk about is always more terrifying than what we choose to acknowledge.

"FRAG OUT," doesn't seem to have had the colloquial staying power that "fire in the hole" has. But *fire in the hole* is the moment before explosion, and *frag out* is the heartbeat after, the shards and shrapnel and fragments spiraling outward and away from the blast. The chunks and pieces on an outward trajectory. Everything blowing out, extending away from the center.

HANFORD CONDUCTED radiation experiments on humans. I found the documents in the university archive. Two people volunteered to inhale air containing particles of iodine-131. Employees ingested milk infused with iodine-131. It is unclear whether or not the milk-drinkers were volunteers. In the early days, effects of plutonium were solely tested on animals. But different species excrete plutonium at different rates, leading some to believe there was no way to accurately draw correlations to the effects on humans. In 1944, Los Alamos scientists developed the ability to detect tracer-level concentrations of plutonium in excreta. In 1945, the Manhattan Project administered the first injection of plutonium to a human subject in the Oak Ridge Hospital. Patients did not receive informed consent, and many didn't even know why they were being asked to return to the hospital.

THERE WAS a second alligator escape. Two fugitives were found basking themselves on the banks of the Columbia and in the warm effluent, near the reactors' cooling water discharge sloughs. They died a few weeks after their capture. The scientists were required to report their search activities, and pressure came down from above to disband the alligator research entirely. Search parties scoured the shores by land and patrolled the river by boat for the remaining missing reptiles.

THE FIRST atomic bomb explosion, Trinity, in New Mexico, broke windows 120 miles away.

RECENT CLEANUP efforts excavated the burial trenches of the Experimental Animal Farm at Hanford in 2006. Workers exhumed 40,000 tons of irradiated animal carcasses, manure, and various debris, including a rail car that had been stuffed with dead animals and buried. No alligator remains were reported to have been found.

AS LATE as 1973, some of the survivors of these human experiments returned for follow-ups, still without knowledge of their exposure. At Hanford from 1963–1970, prisoners from Oregon and Washington were subjected to irradiation of their testicles. Again, informed consent—or consent at all—seems missing or nebulous at best for human subjects.

PULSES OF gamma rays from that first atomic bomb are still traveling through space and are many light years away by now. Two of the Hanford alligators, one of which had been irradiated, were never found.

The Fourth Level

Early in the year, I request some author-to-author support from a writer acquaintance of mine. She emails me to say she will not be able to do so, because she understands that I have been abusive in past relationships and have not yet been accountable for my actions.

I notice my somatic response to her message. Reading it, I don't fly into a cortisol-fueled, flaming tailspin like I would have years ago; I don't feel the need to counter with all that I have already done to atone. Instead I remember to breathe, to stay open. I've nothing to defend. I am done with shame.

It's true: Many years earlier, I acted in abusive ways in relationships, and I hurt people I loved. And up until this email, I truly thought that I had been accountable to the people involved. To the extent possible, those situations—once mushroom clouds looming over my life—were resolved, distant in the rearview mirror of my life.

Now, faced with this email, I am confused by the

suggestion that I've not reckoned with these mistakes, though I know friends of friends of friends still gossip about them. *I don't think email is the best way to discuss these things*, the author writes, and offers to chat on the phone. I take her up on it.

When the author and I finally speak, I acknowledge that *yes, in the past, I've been harmed in relationship and I've harmed others. I've also done my best to make amends and apologize to the people I've failed, and to heal and do things differently in my life*. I ask her, "But how would *you* know if I've been account-able or not?"

"I see there being four levels of accountability," she says. First, accountability to the self; second, to the person harmed; third, to one's community; and the fourth, accord-ing to her, "is public accountability."

Just take care of yourself, and the rest will work itself out, a friend said to me back then, when I was in the thick of it. Fifteen years later, I sit on the bed I share with my wife, my cell phone warm against my ear, willing myself to breathe, to push away the ghost vultures circling darkly in the periph-ery of my mind. *That's not what's happening here. She isn't out to get you*, I remind myself. The author's calm patience makes this last level of accountability seem doable, desir-able even. What she says makes sense. It raises questions for me, too, but mostly her framework makes me feel—if tentatively—hopeful.

I try to sound back what she's saying. "Yeah, I guess I've

only thought about it in terms of trying to own up to my mistakes to the person involved, and to some extent, our circles of friends. Back then, the idea of public accountability seemed untenable." The way that my community wanted to address my wrongdoing was itself a layered act of violence with no path to redemption, no suggestion that I might take steps toward possible transformation. I was shunned and excommunicated. As I faced some of the worst moments of my life, I was forced to do so alone. *Back then, how could I have broadcast an apology to a group of people who'd suddenly put my humanity on the line?* "The community response to those events was more damaging to me—more painful—than anything I'd survived in my life prior."

"From what I heard, that so-called process left *a lot* to be desired," she says. We talk for a while about what public accountability might look like, why it's important, and how I might address it. We talk about the harm of shame, and the potential for public accountability to inadvertently cause more harm. "Maybe you write about it," she offers. "Maybe it's an essay. Maybe it's many essays."

Though I've written the subject into a lot of my work, I've yet to meet it head-on in an essay. For the past couple of years, I've been writing notes for a book on the subject of forgiveness and how we come back from massive mistakes, how we repair ourselves and others. For that book, I want to talk with the man who murdered my brother, with a couple of my exes, with my parents. I want to interview friends who've been on either end of an abusive relationship. I want to consult experts. I tell the author all of this, I suppose, in explanation. It's not like I haven't been trying to parse through it in writing to some place of understanding. But, writing about these fuck-ups of mine requires being willing and able to wade back through the toxic muck of some of the worst moments of my life. Sometimes I just don't have the spoons.

I definitely don't want to reinvigorate the pain of the past for anyone I've let down, and unpacking this trauma in writing is something that always takes an emotional and mental toll on me. I also want to stop acting like what happened is something I should live in shame about for the rest of my life. I want to stop being silent about unhealthy relationships, to be able to enter conversations (proactively and with vulnerability) about what I've learned (and am continuously learning) from the work I've done on myself, and to discuss how we as a community can deal with harmful actions in ways that actually model the ways we think we should be treating each other.

At first, I feel a surge of energy to write about this topic. To embark upon a new work feels like pushing a New Year's wish scrawled on a paper boat, into a lake, even if it will only sink into the water. But after a few weeks of conversations with my inner circle and trying to write this essay, anxiety and depression begin to overtake me. For weeks after my conversation with the author, I awaken in the middle of many nights, jawbones aching, heart racing, breath ragged and shallow. There is a part of me that lives in constant anticipation for *them* to come for me. I wait for some thread of this story—this construction of me as a disposable, monstrous being—to emerge and ensure that I stay small, ashamed, and quiet.

I remind myself that the barbaric approach toward in-community accountability that I experienced all those years ago was far less informed than these conversations are now, hopefully. *Those wounds still linger and hurt, are not completely healed,* I tell myself, *but I cherish the conversation I had with the author.* I feel renewed hope.

THE NEED to know about the *What Happened* beats like a mob's chant beneath this piece. But this is not the place where I dive in to examine the wreckage or reassemble the smoldering remains across a warehouse floor. The forensics of these situations are less important than the short- and long-term effects on those of us involved. But a sketch of the events might be necessary to illustrate the echoes that persist today.

My ex, back when she was my present-tense love, and I date for a year before we move from San Francisco to a small, high-desert city in the summer of 2002. I receive my first shot of T the day before we leave. A trans elder friend teaches us both how to administer the medicine. After, we make the twenty-hour drive with my dog and a few of our things packed into my pickup. We come to the desert, like many white people of the past, for our cure—mine, to leave behind the grief of a major heartbreak and the death of a mentor; hers, to find some respite from the mysterious affliction that has kept her largely confined to home since shortly after we started dating. She wants to support me in my transition as much as I've supported her in the endless pilgrimages to doctors in search of answers. We are allies to each other's art, too, collaborating on shows and applying for fellowships and residencies together. *The desert will be good for our art*, we think.

We quickly unravel, though. Most of our small community is comprised of *her* people, her friends for years. She begins to lie and cheat on me with a mutual friend, even though I offer to put the monogamy she wanted back on the table for further negotiation based on new information, this shiny new obsession. She says no and swears up and down that she wants only me.

She lies to me and our couple's counselor. The friend lies to me. She lies to the friend, too, saying that we are over, breaking up, that she has to cheat because I am a terrible person. I try to leave early on, and she begs me not to abandon her. I stay, even though her cheating hurts me. I love her. I want to see through her bad behavior. I empathize with the hurt that she's lived through, and all the factors that helped her to develop these shitty coping mechanisms. I have them, too.

Despite my attempts toward empathy, I become increasingly confused, upset, angry, and depressed. We aren't making much art after all. The cure of the desert evaporates like a mirage of water on a hot asphalt highway. I feel crazy. I am so afraid, based on all the ambient messaging from the world around me—and even from within my community—that transitioning will turn me into something unlovable and unrecognizable that I start to believe that this relationship is the best I can hope for, that maybe I should accept any love I can get, even this love that hurts me. I start to sound as angry and terrible as she tells everyone I am to justify her cheating. My life feels so out of control that after a year on T, I stop hormones altogether and abandon my transition.

We argue constantly. One awful night, she tries to take off in the middle of conflict, and in my saturation of desperate fear and hurt and frustration, I grab her and push her back against the wall of our narrow hallway to stop her from leaving. This flashpoint, white as a magnesium flame, sears into both of our psyches. Everything stops, goes quiet. I've crossed a line. I go no further, but the damage is done.

Afraid, she pulls away and flees. I've embodied the caricature she's sketched of me, brought it to life, fulfilled the prophecy, become the monster: an almost-male thing that hurts people.

After that night, we continue on—the three of us, really—for a couple more years. The friend and I attempt reconciliation a few times, as do my ex and I, and yet—and yet—I keep finding myself in the same place: hurt and lied-to, confused and manipulated, cheated-on and defamed. Each time, her freckled face stares into mine, begging me to stay with a thin promise of love. I hate myself for knowing better; long before she ever sidled up to me at one of my art openings, bright-eyed and flirty, I said I didn't want love in my life that hurt me. But really, I don't know it any other way.

I fatigue any friends who still listen to our drama, but I am unable to recognize it as something I've chosen. I'm trapped in the riptide of this situation, trying to think of ways to leave, where to escape to, when I finally realize that I can ask her to move out, so I do.

No longer a couple, we stay messily, loosely connected. When I finally move on to a new romance, my ex is livid. This seems to be the real abandonment to her, she who abandoned me long before, more so than my ending the relationship or kicking her out of my house.

The new romance and I turn serious. I feel loved and met by C. She's hardworking and mature and centered. She's sober and works intentionally on her healing. Our histories trail behind us like mangy dogs, but we're working on ourselves and working it out. We talk about growing up, and the brutality of her childhood, which involved a lethal car crash, meth, and shotguns, makes mine look benign. I support her in making her creative outlets the focal point of her life's work, and she supports me in my writing. We heal a lot for each other. We have a few troubling incidents, but weighed against the balance of our relationship, they never cause alarm bells.

After she moves in with me and my housemate of many years, I glimpse a dark jealousy I'd not quite met when we lived separately. She stops going to meetings and exercising and seeing her closest friends regularly. I mention this to her.

"I wish I was cool enough to be able to take the place of all of those great things in your life, but I'm just not," I say. "Don't forget about them."

My own demons are tempting to forget. They manifest most in having little experience in how to set healthy boundaries. I often don't even know how to articulate a line until it's already crossed and I'm already upset. I'm triggered by not feeling heard. I also have some shit around sleep. Being woken up by someone in anger, for example, is upsetting to me.

One night after a particularly exhausting shift at the shop where I work as a carpenter and welder, I fall asleep on the couch while watching a video. Sometime in the night, C wakes me up, upset that I haven't come to bed. For her, it seems to mean something deeper about how relationships should work, but for me, it just means that I am exhausted and fell asleep. Being woken up by someone yelling at me is scary, but later we talk it out, and it seems we've moved on.

We both have tempers, and while mine is practically a subject of community lore at that point, few know about hers. One night, our broken parts collide. A friend screens a short film starring me and the ex as a couple at the monthly performance event I host. I want nothing to do with my ex and dislike revisiting our fucked-up relationship, even through the medium of 16mm film, but C is jealous. In bed that night, I wake her up by snoring, and she wakes me up with her rage about my snoring. Startled, I respond with anger. She responds to my anger with her anger. Soon, we are shouting at each other in our bed.

Then we are out of bed. She tells me to get out of the room. I freeze; being banished is always one of those argument moves that lands on me as a brutal last resort (hitting some deep, abandoned-kid part of me, I suppose), but it seems preposterous in this moment. In my second or two of hesitation, she shoves me, ostensibly to get me out of the bedroom.

"Take your hands off me," I say. "Stop touching me."

She shoves me again. "Get out!"

"Stop touching me."

"Get out," she screams.

"Don't touch me," I say, growing cold and dissociated in the center of myself. We're both officially reporting in from Triggertown now. After her third or fourth shove at my chest and shoulders, her angry face looming down into mine (she is taller, and her face is very close), I shove her away from me. She bounces back off of the bed, as if it's a trampoline; she is a projectile flying toward me. And in the blackening blur of the moment, what I think I've done is swing my arm up to protect my face. What she says is that I punched her.

Her hand flies to her cheek. I stop, stunned, and she pushes me out, slams the door in my face. Through the closed door, she yells, "I can't believe you punched me!"

Dead asleep not five minutes before, I'm now in a panic. As a kid, I was punched as punishment and as the punctuation to rage. I was punched straight in the face for the first time in middle school, by a boy who tried to bully me almost daily. I was punched in the face by strangers who hated my queerness and indeterminate gender in New York and in Prague. I know a punch, and I didn't punch her. But in the scramble of that stupid, emotional, too-fast moment, I made contact with her, and I hurt her.

I know she is upset and angry, and probably frightened. Not that anyone will believe me, but I was afraid when she woke me up, when she shoved me. Not long later, she leaves the house and lets herself into our friends' house next door, where she spends the night on the couch.

A friend of mine is crashing on our couch for a few weeks because she punched a coworker in the face on a movie set in LA and lost her job. She is out late drinking when C and I have this nighttime conflagration. Early in the morning, she ambles in, still smelling like beer, while I'm making coffee. I tell her I need to talk and try to confide in her about what happened, but she reacts immediately. She screams that I am sick and need help and threatens to spray-paint "perpetrator" on the house I rent. She makes the rounds to everyone we know, saying she's going to "bash my head in with a pipe" for what I've done. She contacts my ex, who now lives an hour south, to tell her the news.

C and I take some space. She stays with a mutual friend for a little while, and we schedule counseling and decide we want to work it out. I know that she needs to talk to people about what happened, as do I. But I fear the pitchforks and torches that I know are coming, no matter what she says or wants. My words, my wants, will never factor into the equation.

A day or two later, my housemate moves out without talking to me. (She'd been at her lover's house the night C and I fought.) She leaves a note on the kitchen table, saying she'll cover whatever rent she needs to. One of my dearest friends, whom my ex and I housed when her parents disowned her for being queer years before, emails me from college to say that she can no longer support me as a friend or as an artist, and that she would be boycotting my monthly show when she was in town. A tangential acquaintance emails to tell me that while she enjoys attending the show, she will no longer be able to support me until she can be certain that I'm able to be a healthy person in relationships. *What are your credentials in terms of a healthy relationship,* I wonder. *How will I prove to a stranger the scope and depth of a change I have no idea how to make? How would she react in a similar situation?*

Within days, I am a pariah in my town. People I've known for years walk past me like I'm a ghost, or give me a terse, thin-lipped acknowledgment. People question me for showing up to public events and social functions to which I am invited. Others stop inviting me altogether. A few people do stand by me, talk to me, and remain kind and open with me. I try to remember this, though their behavior feels like raindrops in the lee of a tidal wave.

I get a phone call from a friend of my ex, inviting me to "a community meeting addressing intimate partner violence in our community to figure out what we can do about it." The organizers of this meeting do not reach out to my partner C—nor to another friend in the community who is apparently being similarly victimized by her also-transitioning partner—to ask them what they need and want, including whether they need or want this intervention. Though the organizers of this meeting are people I know, including my chosen younger sister and my next-door neighbor friend, I learn that there is a shadow organizer driving the whole thing, a sort of Karl Rove behind-the-scenes: my ex.

Two queer facilitators from the local rape crisis center facilitate a general and relatively unhelpful conversation about intimate partner violence that seems to adhere to the bad guy script, the "he's trying to control and have power over her" model. *What about two people who love each other and come to a relationship bristling with their own traumas,* I want to ask. *What do we do to not let our pasts possess us in the terrifying crucible of intimacy?* C and I attend the meeting with a small group of friends. I think everyone is there to watch me burn. I have trouble staying in my body. My hands are cold, and my guts are a boulder. I try to breathe, to stay in my skin. I am convinced that I will be pounced-on if I speak at all, as if by vultures on charnel grounds. But as the dreary affair proceeds, I realize that many of the folks are more there to witness than to weigh in. At the very end of the meeting, the butch facilitator says, "Uh, we were asked to hand this out," and passes a sheaf of papers to the attendee closest to her. She looks uncomfortable.

I scan the sheet quickly and nudge my friend Ana, who'd offered to speak at the meeting on my behalf if I need her to. "Can you explain where this came from?" Ana asks the facilitator. Everyone glances down at their copies. Murmurs ensue.

"Yeah, what *is* this?" someone—who I considered a friend and hope still is—asks, holding the sheet up.

"We, um—this is not part of the workshop or the Center. Uh, we were asked to hand this out by, uh, a concerned person from this community."

The letter says that there are abusive people in our community, and that everyone should boycott them and their projects until they can prove that they can be healthy people in relationships. The letter is signed "Team Step-Up," with an email address underneath. The letter, we later learn, unsurprisingly, was composed by my ex.

For the first time during the meeting, C speaks up. "What *is* this? Who wrote this? I don't want this."

The people who weigh in on the "community response" to my mistakes are young, white, mostly cis women, with solid family relationships and access to family wealth, trust funds. They all own homes and some own businesses, too, but they mask their class privilege beneath mismatched, dumpstered outfits and slack hygiene. They have liberal arts degrees from private schools and are conversant in the queer-radical parlance of the early-to-mid-aughts: *antiwar, queer circus, conceptual haircuts* (pompahawks, anyone?), *summer college co-ops, anarchist marching bands*. They had seats in the workshops where they learned language that I haven't yet: *white supremacy, radical queer community, divestment, power and privilege*, and yes, *intimate partner violence*.

Self-righteousness is social currency. Those who appointed themselves to judge me have safety nets holding up their safety nets. All I have—my only resource—is my queer community. And they want to cut me out of it.

ASIDE FROM the closed ranks of a few trusted friends and my therapist, I had few places to which to turn for guidance. Anything I read talked about how it was all about the man wanting power and control. *Was that what I was?* The language felt like someone pushing a sharp metal cookie cutter into the amoebic, rising dough of our queer lives together. Too much was discarded after the punch cut. My next-door neighbor had a queer punk zine about intimate partner violence, but it outlined situations that didn't feel or sound like mine. Abusive relationships weren't discussed as something that two (or more) people build or perpetuate. Besides, at least one of the zine's contributors was someone I knew who, from my outside view, seemed to behave pretty badly in her own relationships. *Whose authority could I take at face value?*

Back then (and largely still, even now), there seemed to be only one model for how we talked about intimate partner violence: one person in a relationship (the man or masculine person, typically) uses violence and force to control his partner and gain power over her. He is 100 percent wrong; she is 100 percent right. The relationship is complete garbage, and she has to be rescued from it, but he keeps her from leaving. He cuts her off from her social network, isolating her. She causes no harm, and he harms. He is monstrous, and he needs to be excommunicated and punished. She is innocent, fragile, and needs to be protected. He did what he did because of power. When I saw this archetype, I would click out of the website, fold the zine closed, shut the book.

It would be convenient if all situations fit that monomythical model of abuse, but the problem with trying to shoehorn each instance of abusive behavior onto that single armature is that it relegates one person to the shadows, enables the other, and neither party really learns how to be in relationship in a healthier way. The community that is supposedly the scorekeeper of accountability doesn't have to demonstrate working knowledge or personal practice of healthy relationships. Their own instances of hurtful behavior remain camouflaged, while they all pat themselves on the back as better-than-the-masculine-bad-guy-they've-run-out-of-their-midst.

This model doesn't seem to account for the fact that our responses to these situations in queer community is a result of our violent, exploitive, carceral, supremacist culture at large, informed by the pressures of this world we live in—as are the incidents themselves. It doesn't talk about two marginalized people who come together in a romantic relationship, each towing a giant duffle bag of trauma. It presupposes a narrative of power onto one person who likely has very little, and reduces the other person into a hapless, helpless being to whom things only happen, in effect, stripping them of what little power they likely have, reassigning heaps of it onto the other person. It's not a particularly feminist take, applying this model to every single instance of abusive *behavior* between two people. Yes, those of us who fuck up in this way are responsible for our actions, but it seems disingenuous to pretend that they exist separately from the sexism, racism, classism, homophobia, transphobia, misogyny, ableism, consumerism, and capitalism that is killing our planet and each other.

I know that there were people who were genuinely upset and hurt and terrified by my mistakes, and who really were concerned about their friends, and who wanted to believe that they could look up to artists in their community and trust them, respect them. It is a terrible thing to learn that someone is not all one thing, that they are flawed, that they have harmed. *It is really disappointing.* And it makes us angry, makes us want to see them punished, to make them hurt, too. It is enraging to think that someone would behave badly and not take responsibility for it. But how can we impose a process that has no pathway back to community?

Back then, the biggest obstacle to publicly owning my mistakes was that the accusations were so tied up in my humanity. It wasn't what I'd *done* in a terrible, triggered moment—those moments became *who I was.* My actions became a proxy for my personhood. I didn't act out in an abusive manner reflexively, in response; no, I *was* an abuser. My worst moments became a synecdoche for me. And for a long time, I mistakenly thought that to be publicly account-able was, in essence, to say that the abusive things my ex did leading up to that awful moment were totally acceptable.

Over the past decade, it seems like everyone in queer community self-diagnoses with PTSD (and for most of us, this self-diagnosis would likely be accurate—let's be real), but we don't like to linger on the "fight" part of the fight-or-flight-or-freeze response. Anger is taboo. We can feel it, sure, but we aren't supposed to *show* it. My most immediate, autonomic expression of fear has always looked a lot like anger. It may be easy to transpose the middle-aged, burly, bearded trans man writing this today over the form of my gender-variant, fifty-pounds-lighter, fifteen-years-younger, read-as-female-fifty percent-or-more-of-the-time-in-public past self. But in those moments, I reacted from fear—not a place where much high-level thinking happens. Would it make a difference to know that the moments in which I lashed out physically toward someone I loved were in moments of trauma-fueled, terror-based *fight*? The kind of fight of a wounded and cornered animal?

I DIDN'T see or speak to my ex for years. I hunkered down in our town and tried to move on with my life, and she eventually moved away. As each new social media platform emerged, I preemptively blocked her.

A couple of years ago, though, I was visiting my old San Francisco stomping grounds when I spotted my ex at an ad hoc queer street dance party during Pride. I felt a sick tinge of terror when I realized she was walking toward me. It would have been too embarrassing to turn and run, but that's what my body wanted to do.

"I know we probably have a million reasons to hate each other," she began, stepping closer, "but it seems worth it to have peace." I exhaled, then nodded. But I was skeptical.

I *wanted* peace, not just with or from her, but with all of the people she rallied against me, too. I wanted to move through the world with a sense of peace that I'd never felt in my own heart and body—not as a child, not as a queer, and not as an adult trans man.

"I know that I really let you down in the worst moments. I'm sorry. I wish I had access to a better way to react back then, but I just didn't," I said. "I wasn't holding out on some better way to be. I was doing the best I could with the few tools I had. It wasn't your fault that I reacted the way I did."

"I forgive you. I'm sorry, too. I was just, I don't know, going crazy then," she said. She didn't mention her role in mob justice, and I was disappointed that her apology wasn't more specific. But it was some acknowledgment, and for that I was grateful. I don't think I said *I forgive you, too*, though I wanted to be capable of such magnanimity.

"Can I hug you?" she asked. Though I felt a surge of red-alert hormones flash through me, I consented.

In the middle of the street, we hugged longer than I really wanted to, while queerdos danced in the water that a loud street cleaner sprayed onto the pavement—the city's passive-aggressive way of breaking up the party without cops. But as my ex walked away, I was surprised: I did feel a sense of peace. I thought of all the responsibility we'd just taken for the hurt we'd caused each other. I also wondered if she would report our newfound amnesty back to all of the people she trashed me to, so long ago.

THE THING nobody ever asked me was *why*. *Why did this*

happen? How did these two people get here? Going forward, what do you both want to happen? If you asked why I acted the way I did, would it make a difference to know that I grew up in an environment of rage, constant yelling, and physical violence? That for me, intimacy was the site of violence? That my reactions to feeling terrified and cornered were to fight my way out? That it was the grab of a drowning soul feeling the terror of abandonment? That I grew up being pinned to the floor in a chokehold before school, having to go to the ER for a possibly broken arm, being beaten with belts, spoons, fists, and 2x4s? That I was scratched, punched, pinched, bitten, and spit on—all by people who loved me, who were charged with my care and protection, and who were people that I loved and *still* love? The people charged with my care and protection as a child hurt me, but they are people in whom I invest time and energy in understanding, repairing, and forgiving. In order to heal myself in the present and create the future I want to live in, I have to understand and heal my past. I've needed to ask myself *why* to understand the links of generational trauma that snap together through my lineage, in order for them to end with me.

The bad-guy model reduces relationships and people into totalized crumbs. The entire relationship is diminished to its worst moments. The question I most longed to hear but never did was, *How can we help you both?* And the thing I was so desperate to know was, *How can we help model healthy relationships for both of you?*

adrienne maree brown writes that "to transform the conditions of the 'wrongdoing,' we have to ask ourselves and each other 'Why?' Even—especially—when we are scared of the answer." According to her, this question is "the game-changing, possibility-opening question. . . because the answers rehumanize those we feel are perpetrating against us."

I didn't learn how to be in a healthy relationship by the way my community sought to punish me back then. I didn't even see it modeled in the way that they treated each other. Maybe those interventions targeted me and another formerly beloved artist because we were both transitioning to male at a time when few in the community had much space or language or *they* pronouns at their disposal. Or maybe what happened—both in my experience and in the community itself—was a microcosmic version of how our society treats trans and queer people in general: Time to hit *return* and send the carriage back to the margins with a ding. Being shunned, harassed, isolated, threatened with violence, and treated as if I didn't matter felt much like my life so far as a queer, gender non-conforming trans person.

Buddhist teacher Tara Brach says that we are wounded in relationship, and we heal in relationship. This is another reason why disposability culture and shunning do not work. We cannot isolate and degrade and dehumanize and simultaneously offer a pathway to learning and healing.

Looking back, that sloppy "community process" actually

forestalled my ability to both make a real and genuine apology at the time, and to heal the trauma that underlay my terrible mistakes. Instead, I was busy defending my personhood, busy trying to push back against being cast out of my queer community, busy arguing against the idea that these moments of my failure—couched within difficult, complex, layered circumstances—should become the metric by which my worth as a human was measured. In other words, no matter how "good" or kind or helpful or caring or loving I was to my lovers, friends, neighbors, and community, my traumatized response was how others would forever characterize me.

At that point in my life, my mental health took a dark turn. My lifelong struggle with anxiety and depression ramped up. I walked through my days always feeling hunted and hounded, wondering when the next attack on my humanity would spring from the mouth of someone who didn't actively participate in my life. *Could I trust my therapist if she had some queer community overlap?* I immediately pulled out of hosting queer literary events, stopped hosting visiting queer and trans artists in my home, and closed ranks to a core few of the queer community. My light dimmed.

I spent many hours in therapy trying to process the idea that always gnawed at my mind: *Maybe I didn't deserve to live.* No one had overtly said this, but the dark force of excommunication sure felt that way on the worst days. The message seemed to be that I was supposed to disappear, not only from my community but from public life as well. I could no longer be an artist, and furthermore, anyone who still supported me as a human and artist was suspect—an enabler of abuse. My ex was entitled to her feelings, but not entitled to bully people away from me or to coerce them into making hating me their personal crusade. No one owed me their patronage, of course, but I also didn't owe it to anyone to disappear into silence and stop making art. The idea that I should no longer make creative work was, in effect, an edict that I should die. After all, my creative work was my survival, the one thing that always kept me alive and moving forward.

Before my conversation with the author acquaintance, I thought that I'd resolved all of this. I thought that these flashpoint moments were bruises that hurt just a little bit less with each passing year. As it turns out, these dark places lurk constantly in my peripheral vision, a Foucauldian policing of self from which I can never escape. For instance, I feel like I'm not permitted anger about anything without it being backlogged as evidence of my uncontrollable abusiveness. If one of my relationships fails—romantic or platonic—I fear that I will be blamed. A few years after all of this, I dated someone who treated me in ways that would likely be considered abusive, had those actions come from me. But I felt fated to be there, stuck in a purgatory into which I was born, where even someone else's abusive behavior would count against me, as my fault, because I was ultimately the common denominator. Long before I ever made a foray into adult romantic relationships, I was already branded. I was already scarred, othered by abuse. When people I was in relationship with acted abusively toward *me*, I never thought to name it as such. It was my normal.

I think a lot about friends who have royally fucked up and harmed themselves and hurt people they love while in the grip of addiction. Sometimes I'm envious of the cultural structures that exist for people struggling with addiction, whereby they can heal, make amends, and transform themselves within community. There is no twelve-step program that I know of for people like me, who've fucked up while hopped-up under the influence of deeply entrenched trauma responses. Even the rotten prison industrial complex pretends at providing a mechanism for people who have done wrong to pay their debt to society, or at least it pretends at sentences that can be served and can, at some point, *end*. In queer/trans culture, we place people on our own projected pedestals, and when they fall off, we are swift to discard them. Then we pin them to moments of past failure forever. I'm not sure who will remain on the isle of humans who have made no mistakes, but I don't think this place will be vastly populated. Maybe the Island of No Mistakes will stay in operation via a bot that pushes a cancel button on repeat, while the rest of us hate each other to death.

GETTING TO be the way I was wasn't a solo effort, yet no one else but I could change this. I took my friend's words—"Just

take care of yourself, and everything will work itself out"—
to mean that no matter what I said, it would never count
as much as my actions. I know how angry and exhausted I
am for all of the years I've spent trying to undo the tangled
zipper of abuse from my own life. I never wanted to cause
another person pain from which they'd have to spend years
recovering, and so I've had many conversations wherein I
asked for forgiveness with specificity. To the best of my ability, I've tried to own and repair those moments of harm.

But I also realize that by not talking about it publicly, I've
kept myself out of important conversations that impact me,
my partner, our friends, and our culture. If those of us with
little structural power can teach ourselves and each other
more loving and humane ways of managing trauma and how
to heal in relationship and community, would we be better
equipped to fight against a culture that advances powerful
serial abusers to the highest positions in society? If I cannot
say that I've acted in hurtful ways, and that I'm sorry, and
that I'm learning and working it out, how can I say anything
about the cultural problems and systems of power that continue to harm me and the people I love? Can we talk about
the outer rings of harm without talking about our own mol-
ten cores?

WHAT HAPPENED all those years ago in a small city, within
a small queer community, within my home between me
and people I loved, was a miniature tableau of all we are up

against as radical queers. Perhaps it was a diorama of how we are taught to stay silent about our traumas until they erupt in harmful ways, and whether we use our power and privilege for transformation or for social capital and credibility. It's definitely about how easily we turn ourselves into cops. We want to world-build something better, but we reproduce the culture of shame and disposability that marginalized us in the first place. Instead of self-righteously replicating toxic frontier justice models of a world that already hurts us, perhaps we can try to model the kinds of loving relationships and fair, accountable, mutual-aid communities in which we want to live. Maybe we learn to slow down, to hold and see people we care about in conflict, to stop using them as stand-ins for our own anger, fear, frustrations, egos, unresolved traumas, and deflections. Maybe we stop trying to slough our own shadows onto others, and instead attempt to love others the way we want them to love others.

C and I broke up amicably a few years after the incidents recounted here. I am now married. In my relationship with my wife, which is going on seven years, we talk openly about our traumas, our past failures and wins in relationships, and how to love each other while working through our histories, triggers, and differing communication styles. We don't always get it right. Sometimes we argue. I fear going unheard; she dislikes conflict. I fear that by having emotions at all it means that I'll be perceived as monstrous, and therefore, whatever it was that I was feeling in the first place won't matter. She fears being misunderstood, and some-times takes my feedback as a tally against her personhood—which I understand, having had to work hard to untwist critical feedback from being a referendum on my humanity. I tell her that this is the first relationship where I feel safe expressing my boundaries. I am grateful for the space we create for each other to grow and heal and keep working out both the past and present, toward a future we want to live in together.

NEARLY EVERY day since 1990, I've thought about the man who murdered my brother. *What does it mean to serve a sentence for taking a human life? Time can't replace what was taken, so what does the time represent? What is it, if anything, that we owe each other? Is there anything that I can do to free us both, so that we both may feel like our sentences are over?* I wrote a letter for the man's parole hearing, forgiving him. My ability to forgive him is informed, in large part, by what I believe are the causes and conditions that led up to the moment he slashed my brother's throat. Do I believe he is solely responsible for what he did? Yes, of course I do. But I don't believe he was solely responsible for what got him to the threshold of that singularly terrible, defining moment. I think about the radical queers in my extended circles who would applaud such reconciliation toward a murderer, but who would disavow a friend or community member forever for transgressions far smaller.

ABOUT FIVE years ago, I adopted a puppy who was taken away from people who'd bound his eyes and muzzle with duct tape and tied his body up with rope. The evidence of their abuse is still visible in the strange, wounded pink membrane of his left eye. The first time I met him, he was snarling and snappy, and he approached my wife and me with suspicion just long enough to snatch a treat from our fingers and run away. *He's perfect*, I thought. *I love him.*

Over the years that we've had him, I've seen him blossom under our love and care. He even looks different— softer and sweeter somehow, less sharp with hawk-eyed vigilance. But sometimes he still snaps, like when a strange man tries to pet him (often after I say not to), or when a vet tries to give him a vaccination. Along the way, in his terror, he's even bitten me.

But we have language to understand that fear-aggression in dogs is different from naked, proactive aggression. I see myself in his cornered-raccoon behavior. I redirect him, tell him to shake it off, and keep loving him, keep working with him. *Been there, buddy*, I think. *I got you.*

Throwing a Sheet over the Ghost

"A writer is a person for whom language is a problem," said Roland Barthes. A trans person is also someone for whom language is a problem. And if you are a trans writer, language is a problem not doubled, but squared. Trans lives rendered into literature bump up against the limits of narrative, whether imposed from within or interpellated from without.

Trans literature has exploded in the past two decades. Earlier trans memoir was so important, because it sought to prove we exist. It fought to chip out the form of our humanity and make us something knowable. Early trans memoir threw a sheet over the ghost so it could be seen. It made our corporeal forms legible. But now that the world knows that we exist, our literature faces other challenges.

Tenzing Norgay and Peter Hillary were the first known humans to summit Mount Everest, and there were subsequent expeditions of both grandeur and disaster, harrowing tales of pushing a human's possible limits. But today, now that just about anyone with enough disposable income and reasonable physical health can make the climb, the tale of ascent is less interesting in and of itself, because the uniqueness of the rendered experience is diluted. (I don't mean to say that on a personal scale, such an adventure wouldn't be thrilling, if not life-changing). In a similar way, now that we know trans people exist, it's not enough for us to write to prove that we do.

But even with the multivalence of our lives, it's difficult to not capitulate to the external pressures of narrative and form as a trans writer. If you've been a trans writer in an MFA workshop, for example, you know how your mere transness on the page is enough to dogleg a workshop into an eddy of unnecessary discussion about this *fascinating* aspect of the story that should or needs to be emphasized, even if it's not the central question of the work. What might spark a lot of confusion, curiosity, or a moment of prurient interest in a writing workshop isn't enough to make a memoir *interesting* as a work in the world. Now that the world knows we exist, our memoirs have to work harder. But freed of the need to prove our existence, our memoirs are also challenged in exciting ways to continue pushing the genre in terms of content and form.

Escaping the pull of narrative form is as hard as shucking one's selfhood free of the constraints of the gender binary's false dichotomy. I am speaking for myself here. I write memoir and essays, sometimes fiction, but the book I'm writing now is trying to capture an experience in my life before I consciously knew I was trans. I of course can emphasize what I perceive to be the evidence of my transness—I could emphasize my G.I. Joe doll and omit my Barbie; I could tell you about the toolbox my uncle made me and neglect to mention my love of horses and my tenderness for stuffed animals. I could tell you of the joy of being a child on the beach, flat-chested and shirtless, a perfect bubble that was pricked with the needle of my parents' self-consciousness, allowing all of the shame to flood in. I could tell you of my always sense of not-right, the fits pitched on Easter Sundays in ruffled dresses in a stuffy and crowded Catholic church. I could rebrand myself as having been a "trans kid" and this wouldn't be a lie, but that language didn't exist then, even though I did. For the memoir I was workshopping, the not-knowing is the important part, and the impact of violent death and the theme of being shaped by loss is the story I seek to tell.

But, as a trans writer, I get tangled in the kelp beds of perceived perception. Can my male authorhood tell my story of a gender non-conforming girlhood, where the accepted community language of this current moment did not exist? Does the self-as-author always have to explain and account for the self-as-narrator/character? How can I keep my transness from swamping a memoir that is not about my transition? How can I leave a trail of my gender through the story without making it the thing that takes over?

The weirdest thing to me about this particular moment is how much we expect our identities as writers to carry our writing. In inter-community circles, I've noticed a trend of writers crafting their bios to name every nuance, cross-street, and intersection of their identity along lines of privilege and oppression. Very recently, I read an article that interested me, and so I wanted to learn more about the author to discover where I might find more of her work. I was taken aback to instead find a bio that named her a survivor of multiple abuses and wrongs and read to me like a "trauma résumé."

I spent a lot of time dissecting my discomfort around this. It needled me. I understand how important surviving these traumas—many incurred through the terrible force of our racist, classist, sexist society—must be to the author. Such things carve the core of who we are and force us to reckon with them throughout our lives. I am a survivor of many traumas myself—I once went to see a somatic therapist out of desperation to heal some still-unmended parts, and as a prerequisite to our first session, he asked me to write a list of every trauma I'd ever experienced. He said, "Start from childhood—you know, falling off of a bike when you were five. Write down everything you can think of." I was so overwhelmed by the prospect of this assignment that I procrastinated up until an hour before my appointment, while

I was still at work. I wished that the bulk of my list would be comprised of clean, innocent bullet points, like falls off of bicycles.

When I arrived, I handed the therapist my list: five sheets from a legal pad, scrawled out on both sides. "Sorry, it's long." My face flushed with shame.

He glanced at it, smiled at me gently, and said, "It *is* long, but I've seen worse." I thought about how terrible it would feel to me to weave those five pages into my author bio. These are the events I've survived. They've *shaped* who I am, but they are not *who* I am. And, while they might often be the subject of my writing, they aren't my accomplishments as a writer. Maybe the idea of a "trauma résumé" type author bio makes me so uncomfortable because my own such bio would be embarrassingly long.

But I realized that those aspects of an author's identity are not what I want to know when it comes to how someone thinks of themself as a writer or as a human. I want to meet those details of the author's life in her writing. I want to know of her pain and suffering and oppression and joys and triumphs through the reflection and context of her art. Does frontloading our trauma like this mean that because there lacks distance between myself as author and myself as a narrator/character, my work cannot be critiqued as writing—but rather, it would be questioning the author's very selfhood?

More than this, how might one not succumb to the force

of both gender and narrative roles? Western culture is strung out on the mono-mythological happy ending, the tidy conclusion, the path to transformation that flies like an arrow. For those of us with hummingbird chronology, it's easy to feel a little bit fucked. Just watch Vonnegut's famous lecture on the shapes of stories. He's so right—we love it when a man (or anybody, to be honest) falls into a hole and gets out again. Freytag was able to fit so many tales into his triangular hole because the blocks of tales were already shaped this way. We can set our watches by the narrative structure of the average American feature film, and when movies don't follow that cultural expectation, when an inciting incident emerges at not-the-ten-minute mark, when the music-scored montage doesn't jet us over the mundanity of life, we feel ill at ease. Like something's missing.

I constantly remind my college writing students that, when writing a personal narrative, they must avoid at all costs the grand, sweeping statements and attempts at codifying their personal experiences as generalizations assumed to be true for all. I tell them that although it seems counterintuitive, the more weirdly unique and specific to them an anecdote or description is, the more relatable it will actually be for the reader. The problem with the "universal" in literature is that the universal means how well one's work aligns with the dominant aesthetics of a Western, white, colonial heterosexual, affluent, able-bodied, non-trans ideal. As a writer, I want my work to be beautiful and intentionally crafted and stretching form, and it's less important to me to be legible to the problematic "universal."

A trans body in a trans memoir is under a tremendous amount of pressure to settle upon a clear point, meted out along a socially constructed expectation, in order to be legible to the reader. It can feel like the trans body can only be legible to the non-trans reader if we write to fit their expectation of how we don't fit in our own skins. The interpellated chronology then enforces a binary experience of gender: *I was this, and now I am that.* The truth of me is perceived in opposites, when more accurately the truth of me might be charted along a Möbius strip.

Our duty as trans people writing memoir in this time is to resist and reject narrative forms and chronologies that limit the diversity of our multivalent bodies and lives. For this to work, we have to write fearlessly and non-didactically, and expect our non-trans readers to grab a handrail and to hold on for the ride. I have faith that if we trust non-trans readers to work harder to find the legibility of trans lives in our literature, they will hang on with us until the end.

AUTHOR NOTES

An earlier version of "A Trans Body's Path in Eight Folds" was published in *The Kenyon Review Online*, Summer 2016.

An earlier version of "Lincoln Street" was published in the zine *Thriftstore Troubadour*, High-Octane/Town Pump Press, 2003.

A version of "Boombox" was originally published in the literary journal *Matrix Magazine* in 2016.

Versions of "Prayer for the Workingman" and "Identity Poem" were first published as part of a folio of my poems in an anthology called Qs, edited by Sarah Faith Gottesdiener, of Publication Studio, 2012.

A version of "The Conversation" was first published in *From the Inside Out: Radical Gender Transformation FTM And Beyond*, edited by Morty Diamond, of Manic D Press, San Francisco, in 2004. A quote from this piece has taken on a life of its own as a Tumblr and Internet meme.

An excerpt of "Lips like Elvis" was originally published in *Plasm Magazine*, Issue #16, in 1997 and a version of the full text was first published in the zine *Ramblin' Man*, High-Octane/Town Pump Press, in 1998.

A version of "In This Dungeon, All of the Prisoners Are Free to Leave" was first published in *Trans/Love, Radical Sex, Love & Relationships Beyond the Gender Binary*, edited by Morty Diamond, Manic D Press in 2011.

"The First Time" was originally published as a zine from High-Octane/Town Pump Press in 2004.

A version of "Lessons from the Locker Room" was originally published in *Original Plumbing Magazine, The Health Issue #3*, in Spring 2010.

An earlier version of "Pigeon Hunters" was published in *Cavalcade Literary Journal* in 2012.

A version of "Splinters" was first published in *Unshod Quills – A Pandemic Journal of Arts and Letters*, Issue Two, in September 2011 and republished in *Provocateur Literary Magazine*, Issue One, in 2013.

An earlier version of "Trans Grit" was published in *The Remedy: Essays on Queer Health Issues*, ed. Zena Sharman, from Arsenal Pulp Press in 2016; winner of the 2017 Lambda Literary Award for Nonfiction.

An earlier version of "Holding on with Both Hands" was originally published as "My Pullups Parable" in *Original Plumbing, #10–the Jock Issue*, in November 2012.

A version of "Man Pageant, Unscripted" was published as a feature article in *The Rumpus* by then-*CNF* editor Roxane Gay in 2012.

A version of "My Life in Ink" was published in *Sister Spit: Writing, Rants and Reminiscence from the Road*, ed. Michelle Tea, City Lights Books, in 2012.

A version of "Antoinette, for Example" was originally published as an editor's choice selection in *Nailed Magazine*, in January 2016.

A version of "The Love That Remains" was first published in *A Herstory of Transmasculine Identities: An Annotated Anthology*, ed. Michael Brown, in 2016.

"Car Crash on Interstate 5" is adapted from a live performance at Slant Storytelling, an unscripted queer storytelling at Mississippi Studios in Portland, Oregon, on December 10, 2016—two years exactly to the date of the crash.

A version of "Soil, Shit, and Compost" was published in the anthology *Transcending: Trans Buddhist Voices*, eds. Kevin Manders and Elizabeth Marston, in 2019.

A version of "Half as Sensitive" was first published in *The Malahat Review* in January 2019 and was nominated by the journal for a Canadian National Magazine Award in Personal Journalism.

A version of "Throwing a Sheet over the Ghost" was delivered as a paper at AWP Los Angeles 2016, on a panel called "Trans Memoir—Resisting Literary Tropes and Narrative Narcissism," which was organized and moderated by Everett Maroon.

A NOTE ON LANGUAGE

About the title: The concept of *passing* in American culture has a long and fraught history, most notably along lines of race, class, religion, ethnicity, and immigration. "Passing" is a complicated and multivalent issue in the lives of many trans people, for whom it is assumed by cis-hetero patriarchy that to "pass" as their identified gender is the goal. The flip side of this is that our culture exacts a particularly terrible toll on those trans people who do not "pass" or who do not want to "pass" or who can't "pass." Early on in my transition, I'd go on long road rides on my forty-dollar bicycle through the small mountain villages surrounding Santa Fe, New Mexico. In the valley town of Galisteo, I'd ride past yellow signs along the narrow, two-lane highway that weaved between ranches and desert that said, "Pass with Care." These signs seemed like an excoriation, or at least an unsubtle provocation for me to really examine what it would mean to step into the visible role of a white man in America in my very near future. The road signs seemed like good advice. These essays map just some of those investigations.

About trans taxonomy and vernacular: Language changes over time. Our conversations about what we call ourselves and our bodies as people along a trans/gender-non-conforming spectrum have increased exponentially in just the past few years, and I suspect they will continue to multiply and to expand. This is a good thing. In my mind, movement toward a near future where things are more expansive, more inclusive, more just, more layered and complex is a good thing. This encapsulates the heart of my politics: If we are fighting for more peace, inclusivity, and justice for all people (as well as for the land, the water, the air, and the living creatures that depend on all of these elementals in their unsullied state to survive), then we are going in the right direction. If politics aims toward the opposite—a drawing of lines, a cutting-out, an *othering*—then it needs immediate reevaluation.

In some places I have chosen to keep trans vernacular as I originally wrote it ten or twenty years ago, for several reasons. One, I want to honor the different identities that I've inhabited over time. For example, my early gender identity as butch was, and remains, incredibly important to me in terms of how I conceive of masculinity and gender in general. Butch/femme queer identity has a long and important history, not only in terms of queer gender and sexuality, but also in terms of class and culture. Butch/femme remains an important touchstone for my desires, even now. Another reason I kept some instances of language that we may no longer consider current nor entirely fashionable or even "correct" is because *to edit all of it out is an erasure of trans history:* mine and the people of my interwoven communities. I believe in keeping things complex—especially language and identity. While I will do my level best to refer to people with the terms and pronouns that make them feel seen and respected, *I also assert my right to do the same for myself.* To erase the language that my peers and heroes and I once (or maybe even still) use to describe ourselves is to continue to exact the toll of the tactics of white colonization and gentrification that consumes our culture onto the bodies and identities of each other.

Finally, I kept some language the same because *this book is for us,* and I trust us and our skills in code-switching and knowing the difference between language for *us,* that we use among ourselves, the language we use "out there" to get our needs met in various ways, and the places of overlap and fluctuation between the two. For example, I think about how in 2001, I used language to describe a "trapped in the wrong body" narrative to get my first T script from a doctor; a few years later, I wrote a letter to my huge extended family referring to my identity as a DSM diagnosis—something I've never, ever agreed with, but I felt that giving my relatives the framework of my transness as a medicalized condition would help them to understand that my gender was not a hobby or a "lifestyle choice."

On the other hand, I've had people call me "they," which is, in fact, a misgendering, and I've had people decide without asking me that I'm a "binary trans man," which is also, in a sense, a misgendering. To label me binary erases my history, my experience, my daily navigation of this cis-het patriarchy, and the realities of my physical body. To call me "they" is to erase how terrible it felt to be called "she," how terrifying it was to ask people to call me "he," and also, how healing it was to finally be referred to with the pronoun that felt, and was, correct for me. If we need and want people to ask us about and to understand the language that we use for ourselves, we shouldn't then jump to conclusions about what living in a body *means* for another trans person without asking. The language I use for myself, my identity, and my body with my lovers and closest people differs in some respects from what might I say when giving a lecture or doing a trans awareness training. As an educator, I often ask my university students to extend generosity and compassion to our queer/trans forebears when we engage with their work, especially if they use language for themselves and their bodies and lives that we might not feel comfortable using for own selves today.

The amazing thing about our present moment is that trans and gender-non-conforming and nonbinary folks from the generation(s) after mine are creating an expansiveness of identity that was not available for my generation in the same way. Our experiences and histories beneath a trans umbrella might differ, but we share a common cause and a united fight for self-determination over our bodies and our lives. I offer these glimpses of my path as an act of generosity and love to those who came before me and to those who come after me: Every single day, I learn so much from you. Thank you.

ACKNOWLEDGMENTS

Being an artist and a gendered human happen relationally. I wouldn't have shared a single written word without the support, encouragement, critique, and inspiration of many brilliant artists, writers, and thinkers whom I've been lucky to encounter through decades of friendship and community. I wouldn't be alive without the trans and queer folks who came before me and made creative work about their experiences.

Thank you to the Dottir team: Jennifer Baumgardner, Larissa Melo Pienkowski, Drew Stevens, and Kait Heacock. This book evolved into a work beyond what I'd imagined possible, thanks to your vision, guidance, wisdom, and hard work. This book is as much yours as it is mine.

Thank you to the many writer and artist friends who've held me over the years. If you don't see your name here, please know that your influence is always felt. Michelle Tea, thank you so much for the decades of unwavering inspiration and support and friendship you've gifted me and so many other writers. Sini Anderson, thank you for a quarter-century of love and creative brilliance. Thank you to Morty Diamond, Carter Sickels, Tom Leger, Riley Macleod, Cat Fitzpatrick, Casey Plett, T Cooper, Ryka Aoki, Colette Arrand, Brook Shelley, Grace Reynolds, Everett Maroon, A.M. O'Malley-Miller, Mattilda Bernstein Sycamore, Natalia Vigil, Trace Peterson, Celeste Chan, Samiya Bashir, Annie Sprinkle, Beth Stephens, Alysia Angel, Andrea Lawlor, Kathe Izzo, Felice Shays, Gwendolyn Ann Smith, ER Anderson, Torrey Peters, Ellie Piper, Heather Quinn, Sarah Marshall, Daphne Gottlieb, Sean Aaron Bowers, Cheryl Strayed, Louise Rafkin, Lidia Yuknavitch, Jordy Jones, Stafford, Anna Joy Springer, Brontez Purnell, Tammy Lynne Stoner, Bucky Sinister, Raquel Gutiérrez, Eileen Myles, Dorothy Allison, Jillian Lauren, and Ali Liebegott. My gratitude to Morgan M Page and Susan Stryker for the compass of your beautiful writing that foregrounds this book. Thank you to Chris Kraus, Lily Burana, Sophia Shalmiyev, Tom Bissell, Jonathan D. Katz, Melissa Febos, Sarah Schulman, Steve Almond, Michelle Tea, and Carter Sickels for your words of support.

My appreciation to all of the editors who engaged with and published my work in various contexts: Ames Hawkins, Candace Eros Diaz, Zena Sharman, Roxane Gay, Monet Thomas, Miah Jeffra, Raluca Albu, Shay Alderman, Dana Snitzky, Carrie Seitzinger, Sarah Faith Gottesdiener, Leo Plass, Stella Ryan-Lozon, Ali Liebegott, Rachel Mindell,

William Johnson, Michelle Tea, Morty Diamond, Amos Mac and Rocco Kayiatos, Dena Rash Guzman, Ali Blythe, Trevor Corkum, Betsy Warland, Casey Plett and Cat Fitzpatrick, Cutter Williams, Kevin Manders, Michael Eric Brown, and Lucas Crawford.

Thank you to all of my teachers and mentors, including Sarah Schulman, Paul Collins, Leni Zumas, Susan Kirtley, Jonathan Walker, Abbey Gaterud, Tom Bissell, Dennis Stovall, Carla Trujillo, Michael McGregor, Amy Stewart, and Ginger Strand. For the time, space, resources, and mentorship, I thank RADAR Labs, the Lambda Literary Foundation, the Regional Arts and Culture Council, and the Sou'wester Lodge.

I learn so much about the craft of writing and the vulnerability it takes to write from my students in university courses, writing workshops, and through my Writers in the Schools residencies. Thank you to all of you: I am humbly changed by your dedication, fortitude, and curiosity.

Thanks to Harry Dodge for encouraging me to share my writing in public for the very first time many, many years ago; and thanks to Harry, Judith Moman, and Silas Howard for making a space for so many of us to come together and incubate our creativity, love, friendship, and identities in a little, scrappy sanctuary that smelled of burnt toast.

Thank you to my family for your courage and patience with having a nonfiction writer in the fold. It's not easy. I hope that you see this work as a loving attempt to recast the culture of silence that has shaped us all, and to forge it with our familial love of storytelling, history, and lore. Thank you for supporting my love of reading and my urge to create from the earliest moments of my memory. Thank you to my dearest friends and chosen family: I am nothing without you. You know who you are.

I am grateful to have completed this book while living in Mi'kma'ki, the ancestral and unceded territory of the Mi'kmaq People. My ancestors have lived here continuously for centuries, and I strive to understand how to live here as a white man, guest, and ally under the Treaties of Peace and Friendship.

And finally, above all, thank you to my wife, Eli Manning, for seeing all of me: intellect, spirit, heart, and flesh; and for allowing time and space out of our shared lives for my writing to flourish. Every day I wake up grateful for the project of world-building that we've taken up together. I love and adore you beyond the scope of available words.

BIBLIOGRAPHY

Eastman, Toby. *Larkin Street Stories: Working with Transgender Youth.* Rockville, MD: Homelessness Resource Center, Substance Abuse and Mental Health Services Administration, 2011.

Ellis, Alan. *The Harvey Milk Institute Guide to Lesbian, Gay, Bisexual, Transgender, and Queer Internet Research.* New York: Harrington Park Press, 2002.

Hayward, Eva. "Spiderwomen: Notes on Transpositions." *Transgender Migrations: The Bodies, Borders, and Politics of Transition.* Edited by Trystan Cotten. Hoboken: Taylor and Francis, 2012.

Pandita, Sayadaw U. Quoted in *Transcending: Trans Buddhist Voices.* Edited by Kevin Manders and Elizabeth Marston. Berkeley: North Atlantic Books, 2019.

Rilke, Rainer Maria. *Letters to a Young Poet.* New York: W. W. Norton & Company, 1993.

Shapiro, Eve. "Trans'cending Barriers: Transgender Organizing on the Internet." *Journal of Gay & Lesbian Social Services* 16, no. 3–4 (2004): 165–179.

Singer, T. Benjamin. "Trans Art in the 1990s: A 2001 Interview with Jordy Jones." *TSQ: Transgender Studies Quarterly*
1, no. 4 (2014): 620–626.

Stryker, Susan. "My Words to Victor Frankenstein Above the
Village of Chamounix: Performing Transgender Rage."
GLQ: A Journal of Lesbian and Gay Studies 1, no. 3 (1994):
237–254.

Stryker, Susan. "(De)Subjugated Knowledges: An Introduction to Transgender Studies." *The Transgender Studies Reader*. Edited by Susan Stryker and Stephen Whittle.
New York: Routledge, 2006.

Stryker, Susan. "Dungeon Intimacies: The Poetics of Transsexual Sadomasochism." *Parallax* 14, no. 1 (2008): 7.

Stryker, Susan and Aren Z. Aizura. *The Transgender Studies
Reader 2*. New York: Routledge, 2013.

Talbot, Margaret. "About a Boy: Transgender Surgery for
Teens." *New Yorker Magazine*, 2013.

Rinpoche Trungpa, Chögyam. *Meditation in Action*. Boulder:
Shambhala Publications, 2010.

ABOUT THE AUTHOR

Cooper Lee Bombardier is an American writer and visual artist living in Canada. His work is widely anthologized and has been published in *The Kenyon Review, Ninth Letter, The Malahat Review, CutBank, Nailed Magazine, Longreads, BOMB,* and *The Rumpus.*